Legendary Learning:

The Famous Homeschoolers' Guide to Self-Directed Excellence

Jamie McMillin

Rivers & Years Publishing
Novato, California

Legendary Learning
The Famous Homeschoolers' Guide to Self-Directed Excellence
Copyright © 2012 by Jamie McMillin

ISBN: 978-0-9831510-0-5

Published by Rivers and Years Publishing, LLC
Novato, California

Cover Design by Cyanotype Book Architects, www.cyanotype.ca
Editing by Lorna Lynch

Library of Congress Control Number: 2011900942

For more information, please contact the publisher at
editor@riversandyears.com

Printed in the United States of America

For my parents,
Jim and Barbara Patton,
who always believed in me.

Contents

Part Two — Determination

Acknowledgements

I am so grateful for all the generous people who have helped me with this book. For guidance and feedback — thanks go to Sam Horn, H.W. Brands, and all my friends from the Maui Writer's Conference; also Caterina Maxwell, Teri Mullen, Kathy Wells, and Judy Ruzicka. I especially want to thank the wise women who have supported me through this whole project: Mariane Weigley, Janice DeCovnick, and my mom, Barbara Patton. You are the best!

For moral support, good humor, and patience — thanks go to Lizz Robnett, Kelly Myers, Tobias Friedrich, Fiona Langenberger, Dan and Ann MacNeill, and my ever-supportive husband, Pat McMillin. I love you all.

Above all, I must thank my kids, Jesse, Aengus and EmmaVee for their inspiration, and permission to talk about them in this book. They have been my best teachers.

Author's Note

My choice to study "famous" homeschoolers does not mean that I favor fame for any particular reason. My goal was to research successful people who experienced an unconventional education (by today's standards). Since modern homeschooling graduates are still fairly young, I needed to look further back to find examples of people with established careers and accomplishments.

I decided the best way for me to then learn about these individuals was through biographies. Unfortunately, this limited me to people famous enough to have biographies written about them. I would have loved to research some of the less-famous-but-no-less-influential visionaries, but that was just too impractical for the purposes of this book.

Also, I had to make a subjective decision about what it means to be homeschooled. Very few of the people I studied were exclusively taught at home. Many attended public or private schools for part of their youth. Some did not go to school at all, but were not intentionally taught anything at home either. I decided to only include people here who spent at least two years outside of school walls from the ages of five to eighteen, although most of my subjects spent at least four years outside the system. It did not matter if they were taught by a family member, tutor, or themselves, as long as a school did not direct their education.

Not all of my research came from biographies. I included observations from people who were not homeschooled at all, but their examples or research reinforced my message in a meaningful way.

Chapter One
That Divine Spark

"If you have anything really valuable to contribute to the world
it will come through the expression of your own personality,
that single spark of divinity that sets you off
and makes you different from every other living creature."

—Bruce Barton

"This – is – so – stupid!" Jesse stabbed his pencil into the math book with each word. "I hate this!"

I waited. There was no point in saying anything when he got like this. He drew a scowling face deep into the paper. He drew smoke coming out of the ears, then jagged lightning bolts reaching out to obliterate the nearby fractions. This was the third math book I had tried with Jesse. No amount of colorful pictures, or white space, or friendly diagrams seemed to penetrate his fear and loathing of math. My usual remedy for this sort of mutiny was to rush to my bookshelf and find a book to tell me what to do. But I'd already read all the books. I only had one idea left.

"So, Jesse," I said, "you don't seem to like this book much."

"NO! I hate it!"

"Well, what do you think would be a better way to learn math?"

He stopped pencil-slashing the page and leaned back in his chair. "Games," he answered. "I like games better."

"OK," I agreed. And that's what he got. For the next three years, we played every manner of math game I could devise or find. He was happy, but I was worried. It was hard to find games to cover every concept. What if he missed something? What if I was messing up his whole life?

Advocates of "Child-Led Learning" told me that eight-year-old Jesse would learn best in his own way and on his own timetable. "Classical" homeschoolers would say that he should be doing every single problem of the Saxon textbook because "Children need constant review and repetition." Who was right?

It's hard enough on homeschoolers to believe we are doing the right thing by not sending our kids to school. But then we have the added burden of choosing the right "how" to teach our kids. New homeschooling parents canvass their more experienced acquaintances with anxious questions like, "What curriculum do you use?" and, "What do you do all day?" Then they must sort through all the different answers and look up various recommendations on the Internet. They all figure it out eventually, sometimes trying a number of different methods before settling on one.

But I was not content with short-term solutions. I wanted to take a longer view—not just "Which curriculum should I use?" but "What am I aiming for?" My ultimate goal was for my kids to reach their fullest potential and lead happy, productive lives. But most books about homeschooling and education seem to stop with college, as if that were the only milestone that matters. I wanted to know how our homeschooling decisions now might affect their success twenty, thirty, or forty years down the road.

Fortunately, we're not the first people on Earth to teach our children at home. I had seen a list floating around the web of "Famous Homeschoolers." Here were scientists, artists, presidents, inventors, and many others who had all been taught at home for at least part of their childhoods. Did any of them skip math? Did any of them throw pencils across the room? I would have loved to invite Robert Frost's mother over for lunch and ask her how she managed. Whatever she did, it was good enough. Robert Frost may not be known for his mathematical acumen, but he was an astounding poet. How did that happen? What could Mrs. Frost, or Mrs. Edison, or Mrs. Patton teach me about raising my own children? The only place to turn was more books.

What does it mean to be successful?

Success can mean different things to different people: college degree, financial stability, fame, respectability, happiness, piety, power, wealth, or perhaps contribution to society. For the purposes of this book though, my definition of success is bringing forth the best that is in you—that one unique vision of truth that is itching to be expressed. Whether accountant or artist, the successful person manifests his or her full creative energies.

There have been countless successful people over the centuries who never became wildly famous and never had biographies written about them (our loss). Likewise, there have been plenty of scoundrels who become famous for the wrong reasons. By choosing to research famous subjects in this book, I do not mean to imply that fame equals success, only that famous people are easier to research.

I made up a long list of questions and set about the task of researching famous homeschoolers: Andrew Carnegie, Pearl Buck, Thomas Edison, Teddy Roosevelt, Andrew Wyeth, Margaret Mead, George Patton . . . My plan was to learn about successful people from all types of careers and see what their childhoods had in common. At first, I was mostly interested in how they learned and lived, what their parents were like, and how all of that translated into their chosen professions. Maybe some biographer would even tell me what curriculum they used and what they did all day!

> *"Success is not the key to happiness. Happiness is the key to success. If you love what you are doing, you will be successful."*
> —Albert Schweitzer

Warm . . . Warmer . . . Hot!

It soon became apparent, though, that the search for some perfect teaching method was a red herring. But in the process of chasing it I found my true quarry—the roots of success. Many authors before me have analyzed success strategies in business and life, but rarely have these principles been traced back to childhood. True, there have been plenty of books written on parenting and education; but the goal of these books seems to be getting kids to do the things adults want them to do or achieve some short-term success like better behavior, straight A's, or more self-confidence. What about helping kids achieve their dreams?

I think many homeschoolers make the mistake of not thinking big enough. Their only goal may be to "keep up with the kids in school" or "make sure my kids do well on tests" or "get into college." Those are all fine short-term goals, but how about something audacious like: "My kids are going to rock the universe"? I don't mean some creepy *Manchurian Candidate* scenario where you use your kids to take over the world. I mean letting your kids find their own creative genius to bring forth the best that is in them. Everybody has this potential. Everybody has a "divine spark" inside just waiting for a chance to let loose and do something great.

It all starts with two very important things: passion and determination. The people I studied were not unusually intelligent or talented, but they each found something to captivate their imagination and then poured themselves into it. This may sound cliché. We've all heard the advice to "Work hard," "Put your heart into it," or "Try, Try Again." But it's true! I found no exceptions.

Passion and Determination

Passion and determination transform ordinary existence into a productive life full of purpose and creativity. It is the difference between someone who merely works at a cotton mill and someone who ends up inventing a better cotton mill. It is the difference between someone just playing around with the trumpet and someone becoming a jazz legend. Everything my subjects had in common boiled down to these two qualities.

I found the roots of passion to be:

- Self-Education

- Creativity

Each of my subjects pursued studies of their own choosing, whether their parents wanted them to or not. This was not their only learning, for nearly all were taught the "basics" by a parent, tutor, or teacher. But eventually they all became life-long autodidacts. Creativity was also

> *"Remember always that you have not only the right to be an individual; you have an obligation to be one. You cannot make any useful contribution in life unless you do this."*
>
> —Eleanor Roosevelt

important as each person discovered his or her life's calling, for without it, they could not have envisioned doing something that had never been done.

I found the roots of determination to be:

- A Positive Mental Attitude
- Self-Discipline/Strong Work Ethic
- Learning from Adversity
- Personal Initiative

A positive mental attitude is very important. It sprouts from the unconditional love and support of at least one strong adult, usually the mother, but the more the better. Self-discipline is learned from watching adults and cultivating good habits as children, especially as a result of being given great responsibility. Nearly everyone I studied also overcame difficult times in his or her childhood, and the experience seemed to make that person stronger and more resilient to future troubles. Personal initiative is based on the freedom to pursue interests and make decisions, but it is also influenced by exposure to inspiring books and interesting people.

I will explain each of these attributes later in the book, but taken together, they represent a mixture of freedom and responsibility built on a foundation of something I will call "atmosphere."

Atmosphere

Atmosphere does for kids what compost does for your garden. It is the ideal growing medium, providing structure along with scintillating nutriment. I don't mean to imply that there is a single ideal living or social arrangement for every budding superstar, but instead that there is a set of conditions that help youngsters develop confidence, creativity and good habits.

Soaking It In: How Atmosphere Cultivates Success

It doesn't matter if a child is being raised in the Chinese

countryside or the streets of New Orleans, the best atmosphere is a mix of structure and vitality. There must be the structure of a loving family and/or community. There also must be the vitality of real, authentic life in all its messy glory. As examples, let me compare the lives of Nobel Prize winning author Pearl Buck and jazz legend Louis Armstrong.

Pearl Buck

Pearl was raised in China at the turn of the 20th century by her missionary parents. Her mother taught her at home using American textbooks for a couple of hours in the morning, then she had a Confucian tutor teach her to read and write Chinese in the afternoons. Pearl did not particularly enjoy her schoolbooks, and rushed through them mainly to be done with them. Her true love was burrowing into the pampas grass to read novels (although neither her mother nor tutor approved of popular fiction) and write. She knew by the age of ten that she wanted to become a novelist.

Part of her inspiration to write certainly came from the wonderful stories she heard every day from the people she visited. She knew everyone in her community and spoke Chinese fluently. She loved to listen to the troubles and stories of the farmers and shopkeepers and old wives. She thrived in this rich atmosphere of warmth, community, and stability. Pearl wrote about her childhood:

> Looking back, I see my life in parts, each part fitting into the age in which I lived. If my childhood was different from that of other children of my time, and it was very different, then the deepest difference was that I always knew that I was a mere leaf in the gathering storm to come. Yet day by day I had plenty of love and kindness and I knew no personal unhap-

piness. There were no pressures on me, I had hours for myself and blessed freedom, for my parents were lenient and understanding.[1]

Her parents may have been lenient and understanding, but they were also very disciplined. They observed both American and Chinese customs and had a great respect for the Chinese people. Her father prayed for an hour before breakfast every morning, then expected everyone to be washed and dressed, waiting for him at the breakfast table. They ate wholesome simple foods with seasonal produce, eggs, whole grain porridge, and breads. Her mother was very particular about the food they ate and how it was prepared because of the constant threat of disease. She also insisted on teaching Pearl the household arts of sewing, knitting, embroidery, crocheting, lacework and cooking/baking. Pearl was not anxious to practice these skills at the time, but later was very glad her mother had taught her.

> Pearl Buck
> 1892 - 1973
> *First American woman
> to win the Nobel Prize in
> Literature*

The family had Chinese servants to help with the housework, but Pearl was taught to be responsible for helping her neighbors. She brought food to those in need and became very sensitive to the political unrest and plight of her adopted community. As a teenager in private school, she worked in a home for abused slave girls, teaching them to sew, knit, and embroider.

The curriculum her mother used may have given Pearl the basics of reading, writing, arithmetic, and history, but it was her own pursuits (reading novels, collecting stories, making friends) that helped her find her passion and her voice. It was her rich atmosphere of strong caring adults, responsibility, and authentic experience that helped cultivate her determination to write over 50 books, including the Pulitzer Prize winning *The Good Earth*.

Louis Armstrong

Pearl Buck was lucky to have such a stable yet stimulating home and community, but it is just as likely for determination and passion to grow from difficult situations. Louis Armstrong is one such example. He was born in one of the poorest, roughest, most disreputable neighborhoods of New Orleans in 1901. His father left his mother before he was born and though he lived nearby, he barely took any notice of his son. Louis's fifteen-year-old mother was forced to leave him with his grandmother for five years while she searched for work. His world revolved around racism, segregation, poverty, prostitution, gambling, violence, and drinking. But Armstrong could see the positive side of this struggle:

> I could go on talking about my home town like mad because I love it. I always will. It has given me something to live for. Those millions of memories. Even with those hard times I'd be willing to live them all over again if I could run into some more Joe Olivers [and] those fine prostitutes and pimps and gamblers who told me, 'Son, you don't want to live this kind of life.'[2]

Armstrong's Baptist mother taught him to see Jesus in everyone. He later wrote, "My mother had one thing ... and that was good common sense and respect for human beings, yea. That's my diploma ... I was taught to respect a man or woman until they prove in my estimation that they don't deserve it."[3]

Louis Armstrong
1901 - 1971

Jazz trumpeter, singer and entertainer, popularly known for his renditions of "Ain't Misbehavin,'" "Blueberry Hill," "Hello Dolly" and many others

Despite all the prejudice and backstabbing he endured throughout his career, he met enough good people to justify his overall faith in humanity. He loved people.

His greatest joy in life, however, was music. New Orleans was

23

home to a melting pot of French, Spanish, African, and Celtic (from the Cajuns) music. Mardi Gras, parades, funeral marches, outdoor picnics, street corners, honky-tonks, bars—brass bands were everywhere. Young Louis reveled in the sounds around him. He could not get enough of listening and yearned with a passion to play. When he finally was able to purchase an old tarnished cornet, he pestered musicians to teach him and practiced for the sheer joy of it. This joy remained with him all his life and he continued playing, performing, recording, and innovating until his death in 1971.

Both Pearl Buck and Louis Armstrong grew up in interesting, supportive communities. They were not overly sheltered but met a variety of people and participated in the world around them. They each had enough freedom to pursue their interests, but also a sense of responsibility. Pearl identified with her Chinese neighbors and was very sensitive to their welfare. Louis shouldered the responsibility of earning money to help his mother.

If I could visually represent all the forces at work in their success, it would look like this pyramid:

Passion and determination carry the individual to the top. There's a certain amount we parents can do to get our kids started, but ultimately it's up to them. Our greatest roles are providing a rich, supportive atmosphere; allowing them the freedom to find their own passions; and modeling the traits of determination. I will show you how in this book, using all the stories and secrets I learned from these legendary homeschoolers: what their parents did, how they lived, how they learned, and how you can use these lessons in your own family.

Remember This:

- Don't be content with get-along goals for your home-schooling students. Think twenty, thirty, and forty years down the road. Reconsider what is really important.
- Everybody has a divine spark inside of them waiting to be let loose.
- Passion and determination are all anyone needs to light that spark.
- We parents can help by providing the right mixture of freedom, responsibility, and atmosphere.

Part One

Passion

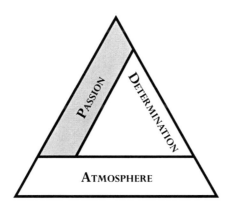

Chapter Two
Wild Intelligence

"Every person of learning is finally his own teacher."
—Thomas Paine

Wild intelligence is a three-year-old little boy sitting in the fields trying to hear the sound of wheat growing. Over the years, his fascination with tone, pitch, voice, and projection will culminate in the idea of a talking telegraph machine—or a telephone. No one else pressures him to study science. In fact, they cannot stop him. A boy like Alexander Graham Bell does not need to be tamed, just supported.

But every child has wild intelligence—maybe not for science, but for acting or woodworking or politics or music. Pianist Sergei Rachmaninoff was considered talented but uncooperative by all of his teachers. They had given up on him and he had given up on teachers. It was not until an understanding aunt gave Sergei what he craved the most—a room of his own with a piano in it—that the young composer came to life.

Bell, Rachmaninoff, Edison, Picasso, Einstein . . . The list of geniuses who chafed under school requirements goes on and on. But it's not just the famously talented types who benefit from the freedom to study what they want. Perfectly ordinary kids, like Agatha Christie or the Wright brothers, who aren't sure what they want to do but love to learn anyway, will thrive when given the chance to direct their own education.

> *"It is, in fact, nothing short of a miracle that the modern methods of instruction have not yet entirely strangled the holy curiosity of inquiry; for this delicate little plant, aside from stimulation, stands mostly in need of freedom; without this it goes to wreck and ruin without fail. It is a very grave mistake to think that the enjoyment of seeing and searching can be promoted by means of coercion and a sense of duty."*
>
> —Albert Einstein[1]

Whether these folks were given the freedom to study what they wanted or they simply did it anyway, the result was passion—for something. One interest leads to another interest, which leads again to another interest. Thomas Edison was curious about everything, but especially science and making money. He went from explosions in his parents' basement, to newspaper boy on a train line, to his own grocery business, news press, and traveling chemistry lab. His ravenous curiosity led him to learn telegraphy and read as many books as he could from the Young Men's Society library in Detroit. He wasn't sure at first what he would do with his life, but his passion for learning oozed naturally into his passion for invention—figuring out how to do things better.

Self-directed education follows our fascinations. It is personal and unique. Young Thomas Edison thought perhaps birds could fly because they ate worms, so he tested his theory by mashing up worms and convincing a neighborhood girl to drink the stuff. No teacher or curriculum advisor dreamed up this experiment, but it worked for him (and I'm sure the girl learned something too).

What Does It Mean To Be Well Educated?

We want our children to have the best possible education, but what does it really mean to be well educated? The number of experts tackling this subject over the years is astounding—mind-boggling. And there are so many conflicting opinions! Pedagogy has been a source of controversy since Socrates first developed his famous "method."[2] It makes fascinating background reading if you have the time for such things. But if you don't, Alfie Kohn took on this very question in his concise little book, *What Does It Mean To Be Well Educated?*

He makes it very clear what education is not: seat time in a classroom, job skills, test scores, or "memorization of a bunch o' facts." His research and experience have led him to favor questioning, problem solving, discovery, exploration, and critical thinking as byproducts of effective education. He basically agrees with John Dewey's assertion that the goal of education is the desire for more education. The true spirit of learning is that creative urge to learn more—to ask new questions, to form new ideas, and to understand.

> *"Education is not preparation for life; education is life itself."*
> —John Dewey

Napoleon Hill, author of *Think and Grow Rich*, defined education this way: "An educated person is not necessarily one who has an abundance of general or specialized knowledge. Educated people have developed the faculties of their minds so that they may acquire anything they want, or its equivalent, without violating the rights of others."[3] Hill gave the examples of Henry Ford and Andrew Carnegie. Neither man had much formal schooling, but both leveraged their relationships with knowledgeable mentors, peers, and employees to achieve their goals. They didn't have to personally possess knowledge if they knew how to find and use whatever information they needed.

Like Kohn and Dewey, Hill also emphasized constant learning: "The person who stops studying merely because they have finished school is forever hopelessly doomed to mediocrity, no matter what their calling. The way of success is the way of continuous pursuit of knowledge." Aside from improving one's skills and understanding, Hill believed that, "The *self-discipline* one receives from a definite program of specialized study makes up to some extent for the wasted opportunity when knowledge was available without cost."[4] [emphasis original]

Everyone is different. We know that. But every day we meet people who have not discovered a passion for anything, except maybe chocolate or their favorite TV shows. They think that sort of focus is only for geniuses. But I say everyone has a genius for something, if we are only given the chance to find it. The problem is too many kids are forced to follow other people's agendas, with very little time or energy left over to follow their own. By the time they have completed a full twelve (or more) years of indoctrination in "how to get a good job and be a good citizen/consumer," only the strongest can remember who they really are.

Children are born with a natural curiosity and drive to learn. The world is brand new to them and there are fascinating things to explore in cupboards, mother's purses, ponds, picture books, construction sites, and playgrounds. There are skills to learn like buttoning, pouring, cutting, swinging, balancing, digging, and drawing. After tackling one challenge, they'll naturally move on to the next thing that captures their interest.

Most people accept that this is well enough for pre-schoolers, but believe that after a certain age, children's education must be directed by someone more experienced. After reviewing the lives of famous homeschoolers however, I found that most of the instruction forced upon them was resented and ineffective. They much preferred to learn about things that interested them or were necessary to accomplish some goal.

Unschooling?

Does this sound familiar? Those of you who have read any of John Holt's books will recognize this as the guiding principle behind "unschooling," a term he invented. After a lifetime of working with children, Holt came to the conclusion that it is unnecessary, and possibly damaging, for adults to interfere in a child's self-education. I have always admired Holt's writings;

John Holt

John Holt was the teacher and author who first coined the term "unschooling." What he meant by that was rethinking the way adults interact with children. Ask anyone what image comes to mind with the word "education" and they probably imagine a teacher standing in front of a classroom or a child huddled over a workbook. The child is placed in the submissive, receiving position and the adult is placed in the position of authority, delivering instructions (or workbooks). It's not hard to understand why children always want to be the teacher rather than the pupil when playing school.

But what Holt recognized in his work with students is how much better children seemed to learn without the interference of teachers. His books, *How Children Learn, How Children Fail, Learning All the Time,* and *Teach Your Own,* are filled with examples of how adults, with the best of intentions, unknowingly undermine a child's natural desire to learn.

After years of research and attempts to reform public schools, Holt finally determined that our whole education system was untenable and that the best possible solution was to keep our kids out of school. He was one of the forerunners of the home schooling movement, but he did not mean for parents to pull their kids out of school just to do school at home. He wanted to stop the whole idea of adults as teachers delivering instructions to kids as students. He believed children needed our help, but only when they asked for it. He felt children should be allowed to learn what they want and when they want, with a minimum of interference.

however, I didn't find any examples of Holt's ideal "unschooled" child in my research.

The only person I studied who had absolutely no guiding hand in his education was the human rights activist Frederick Douglass, but he doesn't fit Holt's ideal of unschooling because Douglass *could not get* someone to teach him, even though he wanted help. As a slave, Douglass was forcibly prohibited from learning to read by the adults he worked for because it was against the law. He had to trade his bread to unsuspecting little white boys in exchange for showing him letters. Despite all this and his demoralizing childhood, he did learn to read and write

—very well—and went on to become a great orator.

Everyone else I studied had some instruction in the basics of reading, writing, and arithmetic when they were young, but the bulk of their learning was self-initiated, especially as teenagers. Thus, I won't classify any of my subjects as "unschoolers" in John Holt's sense of the word. Instead I describe them as primarily self-educated.

I also did not find evidence that any of my subjects' parents intentionally gave their children free rein over their education. In cases of extreme poverty, such as Horace Greeley, Andrew Carnegie, Louis Armstrong, or Irving Berlin, the families were simply too busy working to spare time or money on their child's education. With the budding scientists and inventors, the children often outgrew their parents' ability to keep teaching, which forced them to either strike out on their own (Thomas Edison and Eli Whitney) or search for mentors (Guglielmo Marconi and Alexander Graham Bell).

The Breakdown

Following is a breakdown of the various educational paths I observed.

Children who went to school at an early age, but later dropped out for logistical or personal reasons and then continued education on their own:

Andrew Carnegie	Thomas Edison
Walt Whitman	Ansel Adams
Bernard Kerik	Dave Thomas
John Burroughs	John Muir
Malcolm X	Irving Berlin
Quentin Tarantino	Charles Dickens

Wright Brothers   Benjamin Franklin

Children taught at home for their early years, then sent to private or public school as adolescents:

Robert Frost   C.S. Lewis
Margaret Atwood   Margaret Mead
Frank Lloyd Wright   Guglielmo Marconi
Gloria Steinem   Alexander Graham Bell
Woodrow Wilson   George Patton
George MacArthur

Children taught at home, either by parents or tutors, for most of their childhood and adolescence:

Theodore Roosevelt   Franklin Roosevelt
Beatrix Potter   Agatha Christie
Pearl Buck   Andrew Wyeth
Mary Leakey   Pierre Curie

Sporadic exposure to school as circumstances allowed:

Horace Greeley   Louis Armstrong

Of all my subjects, Louis Armstrong was the only one who enjoyed his brief sojourn in school—the result of being sentenced to the Colored Waif's Home when he was thirteen. The environment of the Home was Spartan, but clean, orderly, and supportive. The masters were like father figures to the boys, and best of all, Louis could play in the orchestra. He never wanted to leave, but was released into his absent father's custody after only a year.

Dislike of School

Of the rest who spent some time in school, nearly everyone thought it was a waste of time.

Naturalist John Muir claimed that he never really understood the arithmetic that was drilled into him in grammar school:

> But when I was about fifteen or sixteen years of age, I began to grow hungry for real knowledge, and persuaded father, who was willing enough to have me study provided my farm work was kept up, to buy me a higher arithmetic. Beginning at the beginning, in one summer I easily finished it without assistance, the short intervals between the end of dinner and the afternoon start for the harvest—and hay—fields, accomplishing more without a teacher in a few scraps of time than in years in school before my mind was ready for such work.[5]

Photographer Ansel Adams had nothing good to say either about his early education in dismal institutional settings. His schools were depressing, dirty, and uninspiring. He thought the act of memorizing irrelevant facts (such as which states border Nebraska) was useless, stating: "Education without either meaning or excitement is impossible."[6] Finally, when he was twelve he became so bored that one day he simply burst out laughing at the ridiculousness of it all. The principal escorted him home for a week's suspension. By the end of the week, Ansel's father had decided to complete his education at home.

Archeologist Mary Leakey had been taught at home and abroad by her parents, until her beloved father's death when she was thirteen. After that, her mother tried to send her to private boarding schools, but Mary despised them. About one of them she recalled, "This Convent's school was large, and the classwork seemed to me wholly unconnected with the realities of life, while the girls of my own age, and even many of the older ones, seemed utterly juvenile compared to the company I was used to keeping."[7]

After switching to another convent, Mary wrote:

> . . . I cannot recall learning anything useful at the Ursuline convent, so I may as well pass straight to the manner of my departure, which involved the customary interview between the Mother Superior and my own mother. I expect there was some thin-lipped stuff about 'Dear Mary is such a high-spirited girl,' but at the heart of the discussion will have lain the well-documented charge that Dear Mary had not merely simulated a fit in the classroom, using soap to produce the symptom of frothing at the mouth, but that she had further deliberately caused an explosion in the chemistry lesson.[8]

Various Homeschool Styles

Of the parents who chose to teach their children at home or hire a tutor, the children received varying amounts of instruction, but the most vivid lessons seemed to come from the students' own initiative or interests.

Beatrix Potter had a governess who encouraged her interest in nature and drawing, but left when the girl was in her early teens because she claimed that Beatrix already knew everything she could teach. Aside from a visiting governess for French and another for German, Beatrix undertook the rest of her education herself, reading Shakespeare and Dickens, visiting the Royal Academy, and above all else—drawing.

The inventors and scientists I studied seemed to have a mixture of formal lessons (which annoyed them) and free time to explore their own interests. But it was the time dedicated to their own projects and studies that had the greater impact.

Thomas Edison

According to biographer Arthur Palmer, when Thomas Edison's mother pulled him out of school, "She was determined that no formalism would cramp his style, no fetters hobble the free rein, the full sweep of his imagination."[9] However, she didn't give him complete autonomy. Childhood friends remember his mother calling him in from play to attend to his reading and writing lessons. According to friends who knew Edison as a boy, he read David Hume's *History of England*, Edward Gibbon's *Decline and Fall of the Roman Empire*, Barnas Sears's *History of the World*, and R.G. Parker's *A School Compendium of Natural and Experimental Philosophy*.[10]

> Thomas Edison
> 1847 - 1931
> *Inventor, amassing 1,093 patents in his lifetime, including the electric light bulb, phonograph, dictograph, film projector and storage battery*

We know his mother also gave him ample time and opportunity to conduct his experiments and build models, and to read quantities of books. By the age of twelve, he had outgrown his mother's sphere and was working as a news butch on the railroad and industriously using every spare moment for running a homemade printing press and a grocery business, working in his mobile laboratory, reading weighty library books, or teaching himself Morse code and telegraphy.

Ansel Adams

When Mr. Adams took Ansel out of school, he at first taught him French and Algebra, and required that the boy read English classics. But in 1915 he bought thirteen-year-old Ansel a year's pass to the Panama-Pacific International Exposition (celebrating the opening of the Panama Canal). His father told him to spend a good part of each day at the fair and continue to study piano, literature, and language at home.

At the exposition, he attended concerts, visited the painting and sculpture exhibits at the Palace of Fine Arts, and often went to the science and machinery exhibits with his father in the afternoons. The exhibitors got to know Ansel and were very patient with him. They allowed him to handle the new equipment in hopes that he would spread his enthusiasm to others. Later he began demonstrating the new adding machine to spectators.

At the end of the year, Ansel was placed in a variety of schools until finding one that would graduate him with an eighth-grade diploma. This marked the end of his formal education. But his true education was just beginning. From then on, he spent countless hours in pursuit of his passions—practicing piano (in hopes of becoming a pianist), reading, camping in Yosemite, and experimenting with photography. Ultimately, Adams knew he could not do everything, and decided to let music go in order to focus his efforts on wilderness photography.

Alexander Graham Bell

Alexander Graham Bell's father had fairly strict ideas about school, which his son did not appreciate. His mother taught him at home until he was ten. She did not allow him to linger on any one subject and concentrated on covering all the basics. But she did allow Alexander (called Aleck) and his brother hours to play and romp in the Scottish countryside. At age ten, Aleck was enrolled in Royal High School. He disliked school, did not earn any high grades, and hated Latin and Greek. But he was naturally inquisitive and enjoyed making things.

Aleck was the poster boy for hands-on learning. While playing with his friend Ben in his father's flour mill, they often got into such mischief that Ben's father ordered the boys to do something useful. He showed them a bag of grain and challenged them to take the husks off the wheat. With some experimentation, the boys developed a simple machine to paddle the wheat with a brush-like material. Aleck was very proud of this invention and the experience of solving a problem. He also "taught" his dog to speak with assistance. The dog learned to sit up on his hind legs and growl, while Aleck would move his lips to form sounds such as "ah" and "oh" while lightly pressing the dog's throat to start and stop the flow of air.

> Alexander Graham Bell
> 1847 - 1922
> *Scientist and inventor, most known for his invention of the telephone, but later worked with hydrofoils & aeronauticss*

He was thoroughly intrigued with the properties of sound and speech and begged to be allowed to go study with his grandfather, a famous elocutionist, in London. Finally, when he was fifteen his grandfather consented to have him, but soon concluded that the boy's education was seriously lacking, saying, "If he wants to inherit my mind, we must do something drastic about this."[11] He started his grandson on a program of reading books and reciting Shakespeare. They often walked to the library together to replenish their books. At last Aleck was free to study the subject he was most interested in— sound. He attended lectures and traveled about the city, the only condition being that he dress as a proper gentleman and keep up with his reading. This year in London had a profound effect on the future inventor. He wrote: "This period of my life seems the turning point of my whole career. It converted me from a boy somewhat prematurely into a man."[12]

Classical Education

A few of the families I studied seemed to follow a more classical college-prep education program. This seems especially prevalent among political leaders and theologians.

Teddy Roosevelt

Teddy Roosevelt's upper-class family was well educated. Teddy's aunt was his first teacher. She encouraged him and his siblings to spend time outdoors, keep nature journals, and write long letters. They read quantities of books and studied English, French, German, and Latin. Everyone spoke French at the dinner table. When Teddy was fifteen, his father hired a young Harvard graduate to tutor all the children. Teddy's rigorous program of study was custom tailored for him in preparation for Harvard entrance exams. He was behind in mathematics so he worked especially hard and was able to learn in two years what would normally take three years.

> Theodore Roosevelt
> 1858 - 1919
> *26th U.S. president, winner of the Nobel Peace Prize, conservationist*

This worked well because Teddy was ambitious and fully expected to go to Harvard, studying whatever was required for admission. But he also had plenty of time for tromping through the woods as an amateur naturalist, learning hunting, riding, taxidermy, fishing, and other woodsman skills.

C.S. Lewis

Author C.S. Lewis, initially taught at home by his mother, was a proponent of classical education. He once wrote: "In those days a boy on the classical side officially did almost nothing but classics. I think this was wise; the greatest service we can do to education today is to teach fewer subjects. No one has time to do more than a very few things well before he is twenty, and when we force a boy to be a mediocrity in a dozen subjects we destroy his standards, perhaps for life."[13]

His classical education did not begin until he was in school at age thirteen, but his greatest advancement came at the age of sixteen when Lewis was sent to study with his father's old tutor

Mr. Kirkpatrick, "The Great Knock," to prepare for entrance exams to Oxford. "The Knock" used the Socratic method of teaching, firing off questions that forced Lewis to use precise logic and language. His first lesson was to start reading/translating Homer from the original Greek.

> C.S. Lewis
> 1898 - 1963
> *Author, best known for his work: The Chronicles of Narnia*

Over the next two to three years, he went on to read all the great works in Latin or Greek, followed by original works in German and Italian. He read French classics in the evening under the tutelage of Mrs. Kirkpatrick. His daily schedule during this time was breakfast at exactly 8:00 am, reading or writing from 9:00 am till lunch at 1:00 pm. After lunch, he would go out for a walk around town or the countryside, sometimes with a friend, until teatime at 4:15 ("Best taken alone with a book."[14]) He would then work again from 5:00 till supper at 7:00 pm.

This type of education hardly seems like something a teenager would have initiated, but it suited C.S. Lewis perfectly. Alexander Graham Bell would have stowed away on the next boat to Canada if forced to endure this routine, but Lewis loved to read and study language. Bell only cared about his experiments and science books.

Natural Inclinations

The conclusion I drew from all these stories was that these children were not entirely "unschooled," but they *were* self-educated. Somebody taught them to read and write and do basic arithmetic, but these skills were just a prelude to the real business of learning—finding out about things, particularly things *they* wanted to find out about. C.S. Lewis was fascinated with the rigor of classics. Alexander Graham Bell clamored to attend the latest lectures on science and elocution. Teddy spent hours hiking, hunting, and collecting specimens. Beatrix Potter only wanted to draw.

It was the time spent in these activities that led these individuals to discover and develop their passions. Each person required something different—there was no set formula for his or her education. Very often, one interest led to another interest, which led to yet another interest. Ultimately, everyone zeroed in on one passion, although some were forced to choose between competing interests, such as Ansel Adams dropping his musical aspirations in favor of photography.

I'm often intrigued by the great differences among people. How is it that some people are fascinated by obscure baseball statistics while others are compelled to drive dogsleds to the South Pole or weld scrap metal into sculptures? I don't think anyone knows the answer to that. There have been plenty of attempts to categorize people into "types," all of which are very interesting, but it is still a mystery how we become any of those types.

Personality and learning style profiles can be helpful if your child is a mystery to you, but your child doesn't need a test to learn what they like to do. They only need opportunities to try stuff. Once they catch an interest, roll—don't run—with it. Resist the temptation to direct their interest. Kids are remarkably sensitive to parents (or other well-meaning adults) moving in on their discoveries.

I made that mistake one day when I bought pocket microscopes for my kids and brought them down to our pond. I foolishly attempted to present a science "lesson" meant to accompany the microscopes when my kids clearly just wanted to be left alone to look at stuff. When I stopped talking and attended to my own microscope, they were suddenly eager to have me see all of their discoveries and form their own questions. They didn't need me to show them what was interesting, and they each were interested in something different. One wanted to find worms, another wanted to examine shiny flecks of mica, and the other was mostly interested in her own fingertips.

In the end it's a good thing we have people of all types to do the work of the world, whether it is farming, nursing, carpentry, or chemistry. But if that work is not a passion, then it is just a job, and true success will never come of it.

Remember This:

- The first step in finding one's passion is self-directed education.
- Children need to have ample scope to explore and experience the world. Their interests will evolve over time and their explorations will become more focused if given the opportunity.
- Parents should help their kids with the basics and support their interests, but without taking over. Future luminaries need plenty of space—they need the time and freedom to study what they will.

Chapter Three
Go Ahead — Be a Rebel

"Instead of a national curriculum for education, what is really needed is an individual curriculum for every child."

—Charles Hardy

Are you shaking your head now? Perhaps you agree that it is all well and good to let children study what they are interested in, but not to the exclusion of other things. Isn't there some basic core set of knowledge that every person should be taught, in addition to his or her own preferences? What about standards?

Let me answer that by first giving a little historical perspective. Curriculum has been the subject of a philosophical and political tug-of-war going back centuries. The advantage of indoctrinating youth to support a particular worldview is widely acknowledged. Aristotle once asserted, "All who have meditated on the art of governing human beings have been convinced that the fate of empires depends on the education of youth."

Ancient Greece, China, Europe, USSR, USA . . . Every political body in history has had a vested interest in shaping the skills, beliefs, and values of its next generations. This is the basis of prescribed curriculum.

Indoctrination

A review of the history of education in the United States gives us one entertaining look at just how closely politics is mingled with the opportunity to indoctrinate children. In colonial times, the New England Primer taught children submission to the authority of the family, the Bible, and the government. After independence, Webster's Spelling Book taught republican values designed to maintain order in a free society. McGuffey's readers continued this republican theme and obliquely warned of the perils of spreading democracy (suffrage). The little books contained moral lessons appropriate for a developing industrial society, encouraging children to accept his or her given lot in life and do their duty, whether rich or poor.

In the 20th century, with a growing industrial, urban society, pressure was directed at schools to supply the labor market. A new scientific interest in measuring intelligence, interests, and abilities developed—with the goal of matching children up with potential vocations. The organization of school systems was changed to mimic factory and business models. "Experts" with utopian visions of a scientifically managed society published books and delivered speeches.

> *"It is easier to change the location of a cemetery, than to change the school curriculum."*
> —Woodrow Wilson

Later, the civil rights movement, anti-communism, anti-intellectualism, humanism, and behaviorism entered the fray, each competing for control of curriculum. Math and science superceded the classical liberal arts subjects in our race for technological supremacy.

Schools, while claiming to serve the best interests of children, often became little more than tools of social engineering. Even the freedom-loving Ben Franklin helped to organize "Charity Schools" in Pennsylvania for the specific purpose of Anglicizing the huge influx of local German immigrants who resisted integration. The schools were a failure however, because a German publicist of the time decried the scheme. If anything, the German community became even more determined to retain its own language and culture.

> "If you meet at dinner a man who has spent his life in educating himself – a rare type in our time . . . you rise from table richer, and conscious that a high ideal has for a moment touched and sanctified your days. But Oh! my dear Ernest, to sit next to a man who has spent his life in trying to educate others! What a dreadful experience that is!"
>
> —Oscar Wilde

I don't question the motive of raising competent, productive people who know how to get along in their community. But I do question our ability to decide how that is done. So many of our greatest thinkers, inventors, and reformers achieved their great work *in spite of* convention, not because of it. Prescribed curriculum, by its very nature, is limiting. It may or may not offer what a particular child needs, and it does not take advantage of those "teachable moments" when a student is clamoring to learn about something in particular.

Reading about the endless tussles and arguments over education, I am also struck by how often the proposed curriculum reflects the skills and interests of the person who proposed it. Plato, John Locke, Francis Bacon, and Isaac Watts suggested an emphasis on philosophy and ethics. Benjamin Franklin favored a practical curriculum teaching youngsters useful skills such as farming, commerce, and mechanics. Quaker leader William Penn advocated a gentle, tolerant system that cultivated the child's natural genius. Charlotte Mason, a book and nature lover, developed a method reliant on great books and nature walks.

Maria Montessori, who graduated with an engineering degree, developed a system dependent on systematic hands-on apparatus.

It is understandable that an artist would have firm convictions about teaching art appreciation or that a musician would feel every child should have the opportunity to make music. Mathematicians stress the importance of math. Scientists stress the importance of science. It's ALL good, but we can't realistically expect to teach a child everything. It would take a lifetime to learn even a fraction of the wonderful things there are in this world.

> *What does education often do? It makes a straight-cut ditch of a free, meandering brook.*
>
> —Henry David Thoreau

Does it make sense to prescribe a course of learning? When we were entirely dependent on teachers to dispense information, perhaps it was necessary to let the teachers or school boards choose what to teach and when to teach it. Even in modern schools, it is unrealistic to expect one teacher to devise an individual curriculum for each and every one of her students. Without hiring substantially more teachers, the best our schools can do is compromise, creating a curriculum that provides token coverage of many subjects but emphasizes the skills most valued by society. Critics of public schools might call this an "assembly line" or "cookie cutter" approach. But proponents would label this "standards based" and call for even higher standards to solve our nation's education problems.

Standards

What about standards? What about keeping up with other countries? Industry and government leaders in the United States are terribly concerned about our apparent stagnation in science and technology innovation compared to the rest of the world (particularly China). In the past ten years, prestigious groups such as the Council on Competitiveness, the Business Roundtable, the Brookings Institution, the Association of American Universities, the Center for Strategic and International Studies, the National Association of Manufacturers, the President's Council of Advisors on Science and Technology, the Task Force on the Future of American Innovation, the Technology CEO Council, the US Chamber of Commerce, The Council of Graduate Schools, and the National Academies have all been clanging the warning bells about our erosion of science and technology supremacy.[1]

The solution most have settled upon is more federal funding for research and development, starting with our lackluster education system. According to the STEM (Science, Technology, Engineering, Mathematics) Coalition of over 1,000 diverse groups of educators, scientists, engineers, and technicians, fewer and fewer American students are choosing to enter STEM fields, and of those who do choose these fields, most are not prepared for the college level courses.

Researchers have been scrambling to figure out what we're doing wrong. One giant study designed to compare math and science performance of US students in the fourth, eighth, and twelfth grades with their peers in other countries is called TRIMSS (Trends in International Math and Science Studies). The TRIMSS conducted so far in 1995, 1999, 2003, and 2007 have shown that US student scores are slowly improving. The latest tests put our students slightly above the average compared to the 58 countries participating in the study. The countries that consistently do best seem to be Singapore, China (Hong Kong), Japan, Rep. of Korea (South Korea), England, and Russia.[2]

It's hard to find evidence that test scores actually correlate with real performance and innovation in science and technology, but even if we disregard test scores there is little doubt that the United States and the European Union are being overtaken by the People's Republic of China. A 2009 study sponsored by the National Science Foundation looked at indicators for science and technology leadership such as: scientific papers published, patents, PhD graduates, Nobel Prizes, and high-tech exports. As of 2009, the US still held the lead in papers published, R&D expenditures, patents, and high-tech exports. The EU holds the lead in overall GDP, PhD graduates, and Nobel Prizes. China currently has the biggest population and overall trade balance in its favor, but the trends (especially increasing R&D expenditures) clearly show that it is zooming ahead in all other areas as well. The authors of the study suggest that the clearest course of action to maintain our world position is to drastically increase funding for research and development.[3]

What does this mean for our kids? Will toughening school standards help American students score better on standardized tests? And if they do score better, does that mean more students will go on to earn graduate degrees in engineering, write important scientific research papers, or invent amazing high-tech products that will save the U.S. economy? Maybe. A lot of people would sure like to find out. The STEM Coalition isn't just trying to toughen curriculum, however, they're also pushing for higher quality teacher training and more funding. These things might help, but the benefits of spending more money on education are hardly conclusive. A country-by-country comparison of education expenditures per GDP shows that Singapore, China, Russia, and South Korea all spend about the same or less on education than we do.[4]

My guess is that the reasons for our dwindling competitiveness have more to do with cultural factors that cannot be conveniently measured and graphed. I think Andrew Carnegie's observation about rich boys could also apply here to rich countries:

> Those who have the misfortune to be rich men's sons
> are heavily weighted in the race. A basketful of bonds
> is the heaviest basket a young man ever had to carry.
> He generally gets to staggering under it. The vast ma-
> jority of rich men's sons are unable to resist the temp-
> tations to which wealth subjects them, and they sink
> to unworthy lives. It is not from this class that the
> poor beginner has rivalry to fear. The partner's sons
> will never trouble you much, but look out that some
> boys poorer, much poorer, than yourselves, whose
> parents cannot afford to give them any schooling,
> do not challenge you at the post and pass you at the
> grand stand. Look out for the boy who has to plunge
> into work direct from the common school, and be-
> gins by sweeping out the office. He is the probable
> dark horse that will take all the money and win all
> the applause.[5]

Carnegie is pointing out here the all-important attribute of determination. People don't do great things just because they've attended a great school or had more opportunities. They've got to want it bad—hunger for it—and work hard.

Motivation

We have no way of knowing just how badly those kids in Singapore or Hong Kong want to excel in math, or for what reasons. Nobody seems to be asking those questions. My unscientific opinion is that raising standards and spending more money is only going to help the students who are determined to help themselves anyway. Kids who don't care won't put in the effort.

> *"Americans have always been able to handle austerity and even adversity. Prosperity is what is doing us in."*
>
> —James Reston

51

Schools are certainly aware of the role of motivation. Over the years, administrators have tried various methods of punishment, rewards, competition, propaganda, and coercion to motivate students. These tend to work in the short term, but they undermine long-term productivity and creativity. This is why better 10th grade test scores don't necessarily mean we will see a corresponding rise in future innovation. I'll return to this subject in Chapter Five, but for now, suffice it to say that the best motivation is internal not external.

> *"As a rule, adversity reveals genius and prosperity hides it."*
> —Horace

The way to internal motivation is ownership. Let the student own her own learning. Let her be responsible for what she does or does not learn. A curriculum chosen by a school board committee is only a reflection of what is important to those members and current society. It may be very well conceived. It may represent hundreds of hours of thought, deliberation, and concern for the well-being of students, but it will always be more important to the committee than it will to the individual students.

I have heard frustrated teachers complain that their job is to teach, not cajole kids into learning. Learning, they say, is supposed to be work, not fun and games. I'm all for working hard, especially as kids get older, but we have to realize that working hard does not necessarily mean learning hard. There are other ways and purposes for working hard until the magic of curiosity kicks in. When children are possessed with curiosity they will pursue it far more diligently than any curriculum might have demanded.

Parental Input

Self-directed education doesn't mean fumbling around in the dark, however. Most youngsters haven't learned yet about the huge variety of experiences available to them or the possible subjects they might be interested in. They don't know yet if they want to go to college or what it might take to be accepted.

I suggest that you approach the subject of curriculum with an open mind, and with the most sensitivity a loving parent can possess. You know your child better than any school board official or teacher. As a homeschooling parent, you are in the best possible position to feed the child's natural quest for learning. It's helpful to be aware of various curricula, just as a source of ideas. You or your child may have never thought to check out a book of Greek mythology or a biography of Nathaniel Bowditch, but these may become unexpected favorites. There is no need to "follow" a curriculum, though. Let the curriculum follow your child. If you know that your child has always liked hands-on projects, then look for more ways he might like to use this talent: welding, knitting, carpentry, pottery, basket-weaving, etc. If your child is musical, make an effort to rent a variety of recordings, or find lessons/mentors/instruments, etc.

Kids who have burned out in school or school-at-home may automatically bristle at any activity that smells educational. They are so used to being told what to learn—and resenting it—that even innocent suggestions such as "You might like this book" or "There is a new homeschool debate club forming" are regarded with suspicion. With these kids it is even more important to back off and let them "decompress" before they can remember how to really enjoy learning.

Gaps are OK

Sometimes a child will want to study one thing deeply, but other times may shift around as new things catch their interest. This approach will certainly leave gaps. There will be things your child doesn't know much about—perhaps the space program or how to write a haiku—but instead they will have learned other things that conventional curriculum never covers—perhaps ocean reef ecology or how the banking system works.

Even if children do go to school, read all the prescribed textbooks, and complete all of their assignments, does that mean they have learned the material? Think of all the things you have learned in your lifetime. Do you remember everything? Or do you remember best the material you wanted to learn—that fired your imagination?

I was one of those children who liked school and worked hard to earn my A's, but later when I pulled out old research papers or lab reports I couldn't remember ever learning anything about the subject. However, I have very vivid memories of learning the things I was personally interested in at the time, such as tracing calligraphy books in the library or sitting at the dining room table calculating the orbit of the moon for a physics assignment. Certain teachers could capture my attention for history or other subjects, but it was hit-or-miss.

It seems self-evident that we all learn so much more when it is interesting to us. And we all have different interests that change and mature over time. Today, if some government authority told you: "Now that you're 36, it's time to learn about the life cycle of grasshoppers," you would think they were nuts. You could care LESS about grasshoppers, and besides, what business is it of theirs what you learn about? Exactly. But as soon as your garden is invaded by chomping hordes, you will then have the appropriate motivation to learn about grasshoppers. Forcing knowledge before there is a need or want to learn, is a waste of time. The time would be better spent on something you care about.

Don't be afraid. Be a rebel. Dare to believe that your child can and will learn everything they need to learn.

It's OK to make suggestions but only if your kids know it

is OK to decline. They may not realize there is such a thing as forensics or microbiology or Chinese calligraphy, but if your instincts tell you that they might love it—try it. If they don't love it, then drop it. Trust them to follow their own interests and you will be amazed how much they learn.

College Prep

What about high school? What about getting into college? This is when most homeschooling parents start losing sleep at night. That's because they still think they are responsible for teaching everything. Not so. A parent's best role at this time is more like Academic Advisor/Coach. We help our kids figure out what they want to do and then find the resources to accomplish it. If they need teachers, then we find online courses, community college classes, tutors, or other local resources to help. There's no need to become an expert on everything—although your own education will certainly benefit in the process.

Preparation for college admissions can be daunting. Nobody wants to neglect something important or fail to keep proper records. But we don't want to become so obsessed with getting into college that we suck the joy and life out of learning. As your child's first mentor, you really need to do a little research on what colleges require of homeschoolers. The sooner you do this, the easier it will be to make adjustments. If your child is the sort who already knows she wants to go to college, then sit down with her early on to look at various college web sites. Here she can see what type of high school preparation is required for admission. Then let her make a plan for getting it all done. She should own it—it's her plan. Ask how you can help. Maybe she needs help finding the right books or gentle prodding to keep on her schedule.

If your child isn't sure about college, that's OK too. Contrary to popular opinion, a college degree is not a prerequisite to success—particularly for entrepreneurs. But do help your kids understand early what colleges are about. Visit a campus, look at websites, learn about different majors. Meanwhile, get your teens out into the world through volunteer work, jobs, travel, apprenticeships, community or church activities, sports or other training programs. This will help kids learn about new things, develop leadership skills, and meet new people. You never know what opportunities or fresh horizons will open up as a result of these connections.

> *"Formal education will make you a living; self-education will make you a fortune."*
>
> —Jim Rohn

If your child is not at all interested in a college prep curriculum, rest assured that many homeschoolers have been able to reconstruct an acceptable high school transcript using just the unconventional activities and books their kids chose to pursue. In this case, though, it is all the more important that your teen is involved with outside activities. I have attended several presentations given by college admissions staff for homeschool families. All of them have repeated the same observation: they like to see students who are well-rounded and have tried lots of things, but who ultimately focused and excelled in just one or two. In other words, it is great if a kid has played on the soccer team, volunteered at the soup kitchen, taken guitar and pottery lessons, and worked part-time at the frozen yogurt shop; but even better if that student can show that she has worked at the soup kitchen once a week for three years, or started her own pottery business.

This shows admission officers that the prospective student has self-discipline and persistence.

If you don't follow a conventional college prep curriculum, certain hidebound colleges may not even look at you. But that's OK because there are plenty of good, enterprising colleges that will be very interested in your student. In any case, you will need to keep good records. It's great if your student has kept a journal or booklist for their high school years, but it will be your signature on the bottom of their transcript. Make sure you can back it up with your own records.

Don't panic. You can handle it. But the specifics of getting ready for college are way outside the scope of this book. Check out my list of resources in the Appendix for some of the many books published by/for homeschooling families on getting ready for college.

Is College Necessary?

The purpose of this book is to help our homeschooled kids achieve their dreams. College may or may not play a part. Even if we agree that more scientists and engineers would help our society as a whole, there is no guarantee that simply churning out more PhD graduates would promote innovation or creative solutions to our problems. None of the innovators I studied went to graduate school. Many never even finished undergraduate studies. Thomas Edison, Alexander Graham Bell, and the Wright brothers never went to college. Guglielmo Marconi, credited with inventing the radio, failed his university entrance exams, but his mother found a mentor at the school's physics lab to work with him anyway.

You could say that times were different back then—now no one can get a job without a college degree. That may be so, but Edison, Bell, and the Wright brothers didn't get *jobs* as inventors. They worked odd jobs first, until their inventions were ready for the world, then they worked for themselves. Invention was their calling, not their job. And what about the now famous stories of Bill Gates, Paul Allen, and Steve Jobs dropping out of college to start Microsoft and Apple in their garages?

There are certain career fields, of course, where college degrees are imperative, including law, medicine, engineering, and most sciences. If your student is interested in these, then he will have to plan an appropriate high school curriculum, but he can still have time to work in areas that are most interesting to him.

Get Out of the Way

Many parents are happy to provide their children with the "best" materials and opportunities but then make the mistake of getting between the child and his or her experience. Artist NC Wyeth is one such example of an overbearing parent. He taught all of his children at home, including the future painter Andrew Wyeth. Their home was described by biographer Richard Meryman as a constant Renaissance school—only the best books, poetry, music, toys, art, and art supplies were allowed. NC's library included full sets of Shakespeare, Goethe, and Tolstoy and all the "important" books of the time. He read poetry aloud to the children—Walt Whitman, Robert Frost, Emily Dickinson, John Keats, Henry Wadsworth Longfellow. Thoreau was a favorite, as was Beethoven. In the evenings NC would tell the children fabulous stories and draw pictures of pirates, Indians, giants, elves, and Santa Claus. He would change his voice and make faces as he read aloud from books such as *Treasure Island, The Hunchback of Notre Dame, Dracula,* and *Dr. Jekyll and Mr. Hyde.*[6]

The Wyeth household was a bit too carefully controlled, however. The children were given the freedom to go outdoors and play, but their father frequently interfered with his own suggestions on how they might do it better. On nature walks he persisted in pointing out everything, much to the annoyance of young Andrew. The father felt most comfortable when he controlled everything the family did, ate, saw, and thought. They were exposed to wonderful books, music, nature, and art (which the father loved) but rarely had the pleasure of discovering things for themselves.

Andrew obviously benefited from the rich artistic immersion he experienced as a child, but he and his siblings always resented their father's oppressive control. There is a fine line between providing a "Renaissance" household and a "Mini-Me" hothouse.

Remember This:

- Don't be content with conformity. Grades, tests, and curriculum standards were invented by school administrators, not God. Those are merely tools to measure student progress against somebody's ideals of productive citizenship.
- It is impossible to teach every student all the things different people think they should know, and it steals time away from children learning about what really interests them.
- Self-education doesn't mean students exist in a vacuum with no guidance or help from the adults around them. But it is counterproductive to dictate curriculum or mold children into whatever ideals of perfection we may have.
- Get out of the way!

Chapter Four
The Barest of Basics

"Once you learn to read, you will be forever free."
—Frederick Douglass

Young Frederick Douglass taught himself to write in the shipyards, watching the carpenters mark the lumber with S, P, F, and A (for starboard, port, fore and aft). He then practiced making those letters and challenged little white boys with the words, "I can write better than you." The boys would ask him to prove it and he would scrawl his four letters, after which the boys would prove their skill by making new letters. In this way, Frederick learned to write all of the letters, using a piece of chalk on board fence, brick wall, or pavement.

Fortunately, there are not many kids these days who have to resort to such tactics just to learn how to write. But it is a good example of how a child really needs help with the basics of reading and writing. Self-directed education doesn't mean a child has to figure out everything on his or her own, learning to read off billboards or shipyards. But when he is ready and eager to learn something and asking for help, that is the time to step in.

All of the famous homeschoolers I studied (besides Frederick Douglass) had someone teach them to read, write, and do basic arithmetic. Some learned at a primary school and some were taught at home by their mother/father/siblings/tutor. Some learned early and some learned later.

Agatha Christie's mother wanted to wait until her daughter was eight before teaching her to read (out of concern for her eye and brain development), but Agatha had her own schedule. She taught herself to read by age five, so her father decided to teach her to write. She started with a pencil and by the age of seven, she was using ink and an italic nub. She read by recognizing the whole word. It took longer to recognize individual letters such as "B" and "R." Her older sister Madge helped Agatha practice writing by making out a copybook with sentences to copy like: "Jealousy is a green-eyed monster," and "Pork pie is made of pig and paste."[1] Every morning before breakfast her father taught her arithmetic. He gave her word problems involving apples, pears, and "bathsful" of water. She loved it and was very good at math.

Reading

Learning to read is hugely important, of course, but it's not difficult to teach as long as the child is ready and willing. The key here is ready and willing. Raymond and Dorothy Moore make a strong case for this in their books, *Better Late Than Early* and *School Can Wait* (which I highly recommend). Their books present all of the studies done on early-versus-late schooling—and the evidence clearly favors starting late. This is probably what Agatha Christie's mother had in mind when she planned to defer reading lessons until age eight. Obviously, though, if the child teaches herself to read, there's no harm done.

The Moores believed that different children develop at different speeds. They wrote: "With reasonable direction and with reasonable freedom, a normal child can learn in *his* way what should be learned at each stage of his development. When he thus learns without pressure, he becomes eager for new experiences. He can absorb new learning much faster than when constantly trying to conform to others' expectations."[2]

Despite what schools may say, not every child is ready to learn the same things at the same time. "Premature teaching often results not only in damage to the child, but also in an enormous amount of wasted effort by parents and teachers who feel compelled to teach skills or facts too early."[3]

Woodrow Wilson, the future dean of Princeton University and president of the United States, did not learn his letters until the age of nine and was not comfortable reading until age eleven or twelve. Some biographers have attributed this to resentment at his father's persistent coaching and teasing to force him to read. He may also have been dyslexic, but his symptoms are inconclusive. Wilson was never a diligent student, much to his father's dismay. As a youth, he withdrew into his own dreamy private world, caring only to teach himself shorthand, a very difficult script to learn. His delay in reading didn't hurt, however, because he later excelled in English, rhetoric, and composition when he left home for college.

Just because a child is not reading yet does not mean that nothing is happening. Children are surrounded by printed words. They see adults and older children reading. They hear stories read aloud from books. They understand that information is conveyed in those tiny mysterious squiggles, and they will someday be impatient to cut out the middleman and decipher it for themselves. Until that time, it is very important to read aloud to children—often. No pressure, no quizzing. Reading should be fun, warm, and cozy. Woodrow Wilson's sisters read to him constantly. If you don't have a book handy, make up stories or listen to audio books. When it's her time to learn her letters or phonics, there is no need to use complicated workbooks and "programs." It's really not as complicated as you may think. Please refer to the list of resources in the Appendix.

> *"You may have tangible wealth untold, caskets of jewels and coffers of gold, richer than I you can never be – I had a mother who read to me."*
>
> —Strickland Gillilan

Even after your child is reading by herself, there's no reason to stop reading aloud. You will be able to read books beyond her ability, helping her to learn new words. Plus it's fun! My kids have vivid memories of gathering around the kerosene heater in the barn while their dad read them mountaineering stories, and listening to classic books-on-tape such as *Peter Pan* and *The Adventures of Tom Sawyer* while on long car trips.

The Best Books

No matter what age or reading ability, the lifeblood of any self-chosen curriculum is books. Stories, whether told around a fire, read aloud on the couch, or read to oneself under a shady tree, connect us to great minds. They can teach us about people and places we have never seen, and stretch the boundaries of our little worlds.

Not just any books, though—but great books. Many of the famous homeschoolers I studied were captivated by the same classic books and authors: *Alice in Wonderland, Robinson Crusoe, Treasure Island,* and the works of Beatrix Potter, Shakespeare, Dickens, Jules Verne, G.A. Henty, George Eliot, Sir Walter Scott, the Bronte Sisters, and others. I saw variations of the same basic list again and again.

These books were so influential because they captured the reader's interest. They were what Charlotte Mason called "living books." If you are not already familiar with Charlotte Mason's philosophies, she was the gentle Victorian era educator and reformer who championed the rights of children in opposition to the brutal school systems of the time. She is probably most known now for her insistence on "living books" over the dry, moralistic "twaddle" that was (and still is) routinely offered to children. In her experience, it didn't matter how much time and thought went into selecting schoolbooks if the student wouldn't remember any of it. The key was to select a *"living* book which finds its way to the mind of a young reader."[5]

> *"My father bought all the books he read and never got rid of any of them. There were books in the study, books in the drawing room, books in the cloak room, books (two deep) in the great bookcase on the landing, books in a bedroom, books piled as high as my shoulder in the cistern attic, books of all kinds reflecting every transient stage of my parents' interest, books readable and unreadable, books suitable for a child and books most emphatically not. Nothing was forbidden me."[4]*
>
> —C.S. Lewis

Mason wrote: "Ideas must reach us directly from the mind of the thinker, and it is chiefly by means of the books they have written that we get into touch with the best minds."[6] And from these books, Mason wrote: "I think we owe it to children to let them dig their knowledge, of whatever subject, for themselves out of the fit book; and this for two reasons: What a child *digs for* is his own possession; what is poured into his ear, like the idle song of a pleasant singer, floats out as lightly as it came in, and is rarely assimilated."[7] Mason claimed that just as wholesome food is nourishment for the body, ideas are nourishment for the mind. And ideas are best conveyed the way humans have always shared them—through oral storytelling, music, art, or the written word. She writes:

What is an idea? We ask, and find ourselves plunged

beyond our depth. A live thing of the mind, seems to be the conclusion of our greatest thinkers from Plato to Bacon, from Bacon to Coleridge. We all know how an idea *'strikes,' 'seizes,' 'catches hold of,' 'impresses'* us and at last, if it be big enough, *'possesses'* us; in a word, behaves like an entity.

If we enquire into any person's habits of life, mental preoccupation, devotion to a cause or pursuit, he will usually tell us that such and such *an idea struck him*. This potency of an idea is matter of common recognition. No phrase is more common and more promising than, 'I have an idea'; we rise to such an opening as trout to a well-chosen fly. There is but one sphere in which the word idea never occurs, in which the conception of an idea is curiously absent, and that sphere is education! Look at any publisher's list of school books and you shall find that the books recommended are carefully dessicated, drained of the least suspicion of an idea, reduced to the driest statements of fact.[8] [emphasis in the original]

No matter what direction your child chooses, and no matter what credits or subjects colleges require, you still have the flexibility to choose the best quality curriculum materials. One of the greatest benefits of homeschooling is the flexibility to choose the best books for your child's unique interests rather than the standardized textbooks sanctioned by school boards.

There are living books in every possible subject a child might want to study, including math. Science, history, art, literature, ethics—all can be conveyed through well-written or well-executed ideas shared by great minds. Someone who has a genuine love and enthusiasm for their subject can ignite the interest of a reader/viewer/listener far more than any piece commissioned for the sole purpose of instruction.

Books and stories are not just about ideas though; they offer something to the heart. Great stories teach us about being human, about looking through someone else's point of view. There is a reason why universal themes such as love, loss, redemption, and good vs. evil are continually recycled in new stories. Those themes are built on human experience and help all of us understand each other better. Kids *need* stories. At the very beginning of life's journey, children are still trying to figure out what the world is about and how they fit in. Their imaginations are fully primed, ready to be carried away to another place and time. A good story will make a child sigh with satisfaction—and hunger for more. Stories that are purposely written to be educational or moralistic are very often not satisfying. Children can easily spot an imposter.

> *"The only books that influence us are those for which we are ready, and which have gone a little farther down our particular path than we have yet got ourselves."*
>
> —E.M. Forster

Remember also that just because a child is offered a great, living book, doesn't necessarily make it the right book for that child. It must capture her interest or it is a waste of time—she will not remember much of it. Switch to a more interesting book. There are plenty to choose from! I have included a list of resources in the Appendix for finding "living books."

Math

The idea of trusting children to learn what they need to know without expert supervision is very scary to most people. That is probably why so many "unschoolers" still force certain subjects—like math. I don't think this is a bad thing, just unnecessary and perhaps counterproductive. You may be able to force a child to fill out a worksheet, but that doesn't mean he or she will learn the material or be inclined to learn more in the future. Unlike public school teachers who are compelled to follow a prescribed math curriculum, homeschooling parents have the freedom to be more creative and flexible.

Basic math concepts such as addition, subtraction, multiplication, division, fractions, decimals, and percentages are fairly easy to teach without a textbook-based curriculum. There are many ways we use these things in daily life: adding money, making change, calculating a tip or sale price, tripling a recipe, measuring a room, planning a budget, comparing sports statistics, or playing games. These are all non-threatening ways for math-phobic kids to gain familiarity with numbers. However, in order to pursue higher math concepts such as algebra, geometry, or calculus, it really helps to have a thorough grounding in the basics. The problem is—most young kids don't care about algebra or calculus. Trying to convince them to finish their worksheet . . . so they'll be able to learn algebra . . . so they'll be able to ace the SAT . . . so they'll be able to go to college, holds very little weight. But an older child is better able to see the path ahead and take responsibility for learning a less interesting subject in pursuit of a greater goal.

> *"We could use up two Eternities in learning all that is to be learned about our own world and the thousands of nations that have arisen and flourished and vanished from it. Mathematics alone would occupy me eight million years."*
>
> —Mark Twain

Timing is everything. The famous homeschoolers I studied seemed to learn much more when they were ready and motivated for personal reasons. Naturalist John Muir had been drilled in arithmetic at a young age, but claimed he never really understood it until he taught himself as a teenager. After the age of twelve, Thomas Edison taught himself everything he needed to run his various businesses and experiments. When fifteen-year-old Teddy Roosevelt was preparing for the Harvard Entrance

Exams, he was behind in required math skills but soon caught up with the help of his tutor.

There are many more current examples in homeschool books about kids who were able to learn four years worth of elementary mathematics in just a short period of time when they were older and motivated. My son Jesse, whom you met in the introduction, is one example. He absolutely hated math textbooks, but was happy to play all sorts of math games (including computer games). Finally at the age of twelve, he conceded that he didn't recognize some of the math concepts his school friends were talking about so he wanted to catch up. He had also decided by then that he wanted to go to college and knew from family discussions that he would probably need to take an SAT test. So we selected a curriculum together and he buckled down—without any harassment on my part. He didn't like math any better than before, but he learned quickly (and pulled down a respectable score on the SAT too!). Timing is everything.

Life Skills

Aside from the academic basics of reading, writing, and arithmetic, kids do need to learn the vital skills of getting along in this world. Parents and extended families instinctively know this and include their children in daily activities. This is how we all learn to cook, drive, send a letter, pay a cashier, floss our teeth, clean out the rain gutters, catch a cab, tell time, etc. Many homeschool books have lists of possible life skills that you may not have thought of, but could come in handy. If your personal arsenal of experience points is lacking, perhaps you could learn new things together as a family: first aid/CPR, baking bread, growing a garden, self-defense, car maintenance, money management, or whatever else seems appropriate.

The greatest life skill is the ability to read and find information. With this, anyone with access to a library or the Internet could learn to do just about anything. In the past, it was very difficult for people to scrape together their own education because books were expensive and libraries were rare. Only the wealthier classes could afford a variety of books. In this environment, it made sense for communities to pool their resources and hire a teacher and purchase books to share. Many homeschoolers still do this for certain subjects like foreign languages, art, and music. But for the most part, we all have the opportunity to learn in ways our ancestors could not have dreamed possible.

So What Do I Do All Day?

First remember that you are not your child. Don't give up your own interests just to slavishly follow your kids around all day providing enrichment. Find ways to include them in your hobbies/interests, but don't take it personally if they show no enthusiasm. It's important for parents to continue learning, reading and improving themselves every day because we are setting the example (plus it keeps us young). If learning is so important and worthwhile, then we should be doing it too!

Children need parents, not servants. Spend plenty of time with your kids, yes, but don't coddle them. Little kids are born learners. They naturally copy us and they naturally want to do things themselves. This is good! Let them help you. Let them try things (unless it's dangerous of course), even if you're pretty sure they can't do it yet and it will take all day.

There are certain things that only we adults can do, though:

• Bring the world to our kids—or bring them to the world. Read them great books; take them on walks; drive them to libraries, museums, parks, classes, and other places.

• Share our time, skills, and resources. When they want to read a book "all by myself," help them learn what to do. Play games, put together puzzles, make cheese, cut out snowflakes to hang from the ceiling, collect pinecones, sing songs, and tell family stories.

There are *so* many things we can do that support our children without manipulating them. Just pay attention to what they like, and listen to them. Young kids are usually quite astute about what they need, although they would not label it "learning." Very often it looks like play. They may beg to plant a garden, or put on a puppet show, or "make something." They usually love to explore, go places, and help with family projects. If a child is in love with dinosaurs or snakes or koala bears, they need someone to take them to the library and find good books to read aloud.

If you feel that it is very important for your children to learn something, there is no need to wait around until they discover it for themselves. It is OK to expose them to a new subject, with no strings attached. If you really enjoy history, biology, or blues guitar, then your enthusiasm for the topic may rub off on them.

As children grow older they will naturally want to do more difficult tasks. Their interests may take focus and they'll be ready to plan ahead for what they want to accomplish and learn. Besides Raymond and Dorothy Moore, there are a number of educators who recognize the different phases of child development and readiness. Most seem to agree that the ages of 11 to13 are a turning point in the child's readiness to reason and take on more scholarly studies. Girls tend to mature more quickly than boys, but every child is

> *"In education, the process of self-development should be encouraged to the fullest extent. Children should be led to make their own investigations, and draw their own inferences. They should be told as little as possible, and induced to discover as much as possible.*
>
> *Humanity has progressed solely by self-instruction; and that to achieve the best results each mind must progress somewhat after the same fashion, is continually proved by the marked success of self-made men."*
>
> —Herbert Spencer

71

different.

At this stage, you will notice your kids becoming more responsible, more focused, and more interested in abstract thinking. Oliver DeMille, the author of *A Thomas Jefferson Education*, calls this "the scholar phase" and gives a very good, detailed explanation in his book of how to help self-directed learners at this point.

I believe the best solution as homeschoolers is to give children the skills they need and want to teach themselves, then get out of the way. My research into the lives of real people has convinced me that children will continue to learn, read, experiment, practice, explore, and create even without someone telling them to do so. That is not to say our job is done. It merely reassigns the traditional role of teacher from director to support crew. Children will continue to need our support and guidance even as they pursue their own learning. They still need help finding the

Oliver DeMille, the cofounder and a previous president of George Wythe University, developed an interesting homeschool philosophy that he outlined in his book, *A Thomas Jefferson Education*. DeMille was alarmed with trends in education towards job or career training instead of independent inquiry and critical thinking. He believed that this eroded the quality and integrity of our nations' leaders. With this in mind he set about researching the education of our great political thinkers and leaders, and developed a method, based on classics and mentors, designed to create statesmen/women of the same caliber as Thomas Jefferson.

His popular program of Leadership Education blends self-directed learning with classical education. The program emphasizes the importance of parents' learning at the same time children are learning. He also reinforces Raymond and Dorothy Moore's message of "Better Late than Early," referring to the theory that it is better to postpone formal education until a child is developmentally ready—often seven or eight years old. If you are intrigued with the idea of a classical education but also value educational freedom, I highly recommend this book.

right books, field trips, supplies, or mentors. Sometimes getting out of the way can mean much more work than just handing the child a prepackaged curriculum!

Remember This:

- Self-directed learners still need your help with basic reading, writing, arithmetic, and life skills. But don't overdo it.
- Don't push the academic skills until the child is ready and willing. Forget what schools and standard curriculum providers say should be taught at each grade level.
- If possible, the backbone of any self-chosen curriculum should be great books, or what Charlotte Mason termed "living books."
- As children mature, they will be able to tackle more abstract, "academic" studies such as mathematics and college prep work.

Chapter Five

Cherry Goop

"Creativity, not science, lies at the leading edge of the evolution of the human species; that is the delightful and beautiful paradox."

—Robin King

When young Steven Spielberg was a Boy Scout, he wanted to get a merit badge in filmmaking. His father, supportive as he was, bought the boy a Super-8 movie camera. Steven decided to make a horror movie. For one of his shots he needed red, bloody-looking goop to ooze out of the kitchen cabinets. So his mother went out and bought thirty cans of cherries to cook into a goop for him. Never mind the mess in the kitchen! She let him move furniture around, helped with scenery and costumes, and drove him out to the desert when he needed a desert scene. She didn't complain about the mess or the time or the bother. His parents helped him but did not *control* the creative process. Steven was the director—his parents were the crew.

Creativity thrives in freedom. It is very personal. While one person may have visions of wildflowers bordering our highways,

75

another may have visions of hydroponic skyscrapers feeding our cities. There is just no telling what people will come up with next. So why are we trying to tell our children?

If I haven't convinced you by now of the merits of self-directed education, consider the rewards of creativity. Creativity is the driving force of human society. It is the seed of all our innovation and the tool we use to solve our problems.

When you think about it, creativity and intelligence are the two skills fundamental to human survival. Baby humans are born completely helpless, with very few of the instincts born to other mammals. We are dependent on adults for far longer because we have to learn everything from scratch. Why is this? It is because humans are born to adapt. Our innate creativity allows us to solve problems and find ways to live in disparate climates such as the Arctic or the Amazon rainforest. A baby must learn to live where her people live. She needs to be a "blank slate" to learn her community's unique survival skills, whether it's fishing, herding, weaving, or web design.

Beyond learning the skills of her people, though, a child needs to be able to adapt to future changing conditions—to be creative. The blank-slate or empty-bucket model of education—

In his book, ***The Rise of the Creative Class***, Richard Florida presents compelling evidence that "Today's economy is fundamentally a Creative Economy."[1] He writes: "In virtually every industry, from automobiles to fashion, food products, and information technology itself, the winners in the long run are those who can create and keep creating. This has always been true, from the days of the Agricultural Revolution to the Industrial Revolution. But in the past few decades we've come to recognize it clearly and act upon it systematically."[2]

The type of work we do has shifted over the last century, and especially since 1950, to more scientific and artistic endeavors. He gives the following statistics: In 1900, there were just 55 scientists and engineers for every 100,000 people in the United States. By 1950 the number had increased to 400 per 100,000, and by 1999 there were more than 1,800 scientists and engineers per 100,000 people.

The trend is the same for professional artists, writers, and performers: In 1900 there were roughly 250 artists per 100,000 Americans, 350 per 100,000 in 1950, and a whopping 900 per 100,000 in 1999.[3]

The biggest creative industry in the United States in 1999 was research and development. Other big industries were publishing, software development, TV and radio, design, music, film, toys and games, advertising, architecture, performing arts, crafts, video games, fashion, and art.[4]

Aside from the Creative Class (including computer, architecture, engineering, science, education, art, design, sports, media, management, business, legal, technical, and high-end sales occupations), the other major occupational categories according to the U.S. Standard Occupation Classification System are: Working Class (construction, extraction, installation/repair, production, and transportation), Service Class (health care, food services, cleaning, personal care, retail, administrative, social services, and protective services) and Agriculture (farming, fishing, and forestry).

The only two industries to grow since 1900 were the Creative Class and Service Class. The Working Class rose to about 40% of the general work force in 1950, then declined to about 25 % in 1999. The Agricultural Class plummeted from nearly 40% in 1900 to less than 5% in 1999.

Richard Florida studied these trends and found a number of interesting cultural, organizational, geographical, and economical implications. His findings are of particular importance to business owners, managers, and city planners; but what this means for us as parents and teachers is that our kids need to launch with their resourceful skills intact in order to thrive in our new Creative Age.

teaching children a set group of facts and skills—is not sufficient. Children will naturally want to (and should) learn the skills they see adults using: cooking, building, fixing, driving, reading, shopping, cooperating, helping, typing, measuring, cleaning, meditating, exercising, negotiating, gardening, care-giving, and countless other things. Some children will learn things that others never will, such as how to ride a subway, milk a goat, or chop firewood. There is literally no end to the number of things a child could be taught, but we must leave room for the new. The present and future problems of society require creative thinking. It is not enough (or even possible) to hand down the accumulated wisdom of our ancestors, especially if in the process we stifle the child's urge to explore, create, and think for himself.

> *"The principle goal of education is to create men who are capable of doing new things, not simply of repeating what other generations have done—men who are creative, inventive, and discoverers."*
>
> —Jean Piaget

Free Time

So how do we help our children be creative? We do it by not squashing creativity in the first place. All children are born creative. The problem is that so many of their natural impulses are undermined by the good intentions of adults. One of the biggest squashers is lack of time. In our hurry-up world, children's days are filled with school, sports practice, music lessons, scouts, church activities, homework, and enrichment programs. Any free time is often spent collapsed in front of the TV. Ambitious parents tend to view idleness with suspicion; or, hating idleness themselves, they prefer to rush from one thing to the next.

Ann Lewin, the Director of the Capital Children's Museum in Washington D.C. noticed with frustration that parents at the museum often coaxed or dragged children from one exhibit to the next, even though the children were clearly absorbed in whatever they were doing. The parents felt obligated to see it all. In their hands was the map of the whole museum and on their wrists was a watch telling them how much time was left.

Children need time and breathing room. Beatrix Potter passionately loved to draw and spent whole days filling up her sketchbooks. But she resented the drawing lessons her parents arranged for her, writing: "I don't want lessons, I want practice. I hope it is not pride that makes me so stiff against teaching, but a bad or indifferent teacher is worse than none. It cannot be taught."[5]

Free time does not necessarily mean idleness. Walt Whitman spent a lot of time lying in the grass daydreaming, but boys like Thomas Edison could barely hold still for the number of projects they wished to do.

Pierre Curie was especially aware of interruptions when he was trying to think. He had a very difficult time concentrating. Everything around him had to be absolutely still or else he had to turn his mind into "a humming top, the movement itself making me insensible to what is happening around me."[6] The faster the top moved, the easier he could shut out the world around him. Unfortunately, his good-natured mother did not understand this, and frequently annoyed him with her attentions.

His wife, Marie Curie, later described his learning as intense and focused. He did not like to arbitrarily skip from one subject to the next. She wrote:

> It is clear that a mind of this kind can hold great future possibilities. But it is no less clear that no system of education can be especially provided by the public school for persons of this intellectual type. If, then Pierre's earliest instruction was irregular and incomplete, it had the advantage of [freeing his mind

79

from] dogmas, prejudices or preconceived ideas. And he was always grateful to his parents for this liberal attitude.[7]

She also said, "Pierre's intellectual capacities were not those that would permit the rapid assimilation of a prescribed course of studies. His dreamer's spirit would not submit itself to the ordering of the intellectual effort imposed by the school."[8]

I believe homeschooling's greatest advantage over traditional schooling is time and freedom. Even with traditional lessons in reading, writing, arithmetic, and other schoolish subjects, a homeschooled child has far more time and opportunity for pursuing his own interests. But there are other ways a parent might squash creativity.

Creativity Killers

Besides lack of time, the authors of *Creative Spirit* identified seven major "Creativity Killers" for young children: surveillance, evaluation, rewards, competition, over-control, restricting choice, and pressure. Allowing our kids to direct their own education automatically addresses some of these creativity killers: competition, over-control, restricting choice, and pressure. But this still leaves the possibility of surveillance, evaluation, and rewards. These adult impulses can be hard to shake, but we have to try. The old behaviorist notions of rewarding or enticing children to perform desired responses have been soundly trounced by modern research.

Rewards and Praise

Alfie Kohn's book, *Punished by Rewards*, explains the current research on how rewards negatively affect learning. The problem is that when adults start giving gold stars or pizza coupons or even praise for expected behavior, a child's *intrinsic* motivation to do the thing is replaced by *extrinsic* motivation. Then when the extrinsic motivator is removed, the child has no motivation at all to do the thing. Teachers are often frustrated with the question, "Will this be on the test?" Implied in this question is the student's decision to only learn what they must for a good grade on the test.

Rewards and grades may be effective in the short term for getting kids to perform, but research has shown they are detrimental to innovation and critical thinking. Children become trained in giving the correct response (the one the adult wants). There is no incentive to think of a new solution or a new idea, because their new solution might be wrong. They learn to avoid risk. If given a choice between easy or harder tasks, they will choose the easier task to ensure they get the good grade.

Maria Montessori is another educator and researcher who had strong opinions about external rewards. Initially, she was in favor of them:

> Like others I had believed that it was necessary to encourage a child by means of some exterior reward that would flatter his baser sentiments . . . in order to foster in him spirit of work and of peace. And I was astonished when I learned that a child who is permitted to educate himself really gives up these lower instincts.[9]

She found in her work with children that the satisfaction of performing their chosen tasks was all the children desired— rewards or praise were only a distraction. For instance, Montessori made a set of sandpaper letter cards with the names of toys on them. She told the children that if they could read the name on the card, they could play with the toy as a reward. The children eagerly read the words, but they had no interest in the toys. Instead they wanted to read more words. Montessori confirmed this reaction with further experiments. Time and again, she found that the children were far more interested in challenging work and seemed almost repulsed by the rewards offered.

John Briggs gives an example of intrinsic vs. external motivation in his study of creativity, *Fire in the Crucible*. In this book he tells the story of Brandeis University psychology professor Teresa Amabile's experiments with creative motivation. Amabile tested 72 young creative writers, first asking them to each write a short poem. She then divided them into three groups, giving the first group a questionnaire about the external rewards of writing and the second group a questionnaire about the internal rewards of writing. The third group was not given a questionnaire. Afterwards, all were asked to write a second poem. A panel of experienced poets reviewed the poems and found that the group given the intrinsic rewards questionnaire and the group not given questionnaires performed creatively about the same in both poems. But the group given the questionnaire about external rewards performed much worse. Amabile concluded that even the suggestion of external motivation was enough to curb creativity.[10]

Besides rewards, Kohn and Montessori found that even praise was detrimental. Montessori determined that it interfered with children's concentration: "A child does not need praise; praise breaks the enchantment."[11] While Montessori teachers do take notes and evaluate children's learning, the children are not aware of it. The materials they use are self-correcting so that children know themselves if they have mastered it or not. Montessori advised her teachers:

> Praise, help, or even a look, may be enough to interrupt him, or destroy the activity. It seems a strange thing to say, but this can happen even if the child merely becomes aware of being watched... The great

principle which brings success to the teacher is this: *as soon as concentration has begun, act as if the child does not exist.*[12] [emphasis in the original]

This may seem harsh to loving, well-meaning parents. But withholding praise is not the same thing as withholding affection or attention. Children still want adult company. They want to have conversations, stories, games, and help when needed. But when the children are busy with something, leave them alone!

Praise With Your Heart—Not Words

What is the alternative to praising? Alfie Kohn suggests: "That depends on the situation, but whatever we decide to say instead has to be offered in the context of genuine affection and love for who kids are rather than for what they've done. When unconditional support is present, 'Good job!' isn't necessary; when it's absent, 'Good job!' won't help."[13]

Before praising or acknowledging something the child has done, it may be helpful to think, "Would I say this to an adult friend?" We would not say, "Good job cleaning your kitchen" to a friend or peer, but we may say, "Thanks for helping me load my truck." Congratulating a friend on a promotion or big event would be appropriate,

> *"All my life affection has been showered on me, and everything that I have done, I have had to do in spite of it."*
> —George Bernard Shaw

but congratulating them for decorating their apartment might sound patronizing. If a friend or child is enthusiastically telling you about their latest project, all they really want is your attention and listening ear—not necessarily advice or evaluation.

What if a child *asks* for feedback? When kids show their latest drawing/clay pot/dance/popsicle stick sculpture/etc. to an adult and exclaim, "Look what I did!" they are clearly inviting comment. It can be tricky knowing how to respond. Animator

Chuck Jones (the one who drew Wile E. Coyote) recommends not giving value judgments (good, great, better, so-so, I like it). Instead, just observe or notice the features of the drawing and take your cues from the child. Let *them* tell you about it or perhaps ask how they did it.

He gives this advice to parents on appropriate praise: "Parental love is not a fountain, it's a well. If you keep pouring it out and pouring it out, it loses its impact. But if it's there when the child needs to go and get some, it's much better. That way it's not what you need in your love for children, but what they need in their love for you."[14]

Did you ever read *Anne of Green Gables* by L.M. Montgomery? Old Matthew Cuthbert, the gentle man who adopted Anne, was a great example of how to support a child, with no other agenda but adoration. He was the well of love that Anne could go to, sobbing or chattering. With few words of his own, Matthew listened closely to her stories, and in the end Anne would be satisfied. His attention and smiles told her that she was worthy and loved. She didn't need praise (although I'm sure Anne's character would have appreciated any praise that came her way).

Of course, this is a fictional story, but don't we all wish to have a Matthew Cuthbert of our own? Someone who loves us completely, but doesn't judge, happy to hear whatever we come up with next.

Freedom of Choice

Creativity thrives in freedom—free time, freedom from evaluation, and freedom from too much control. There's the big question: how much control? Matthew didn't try to control Anne, but his sister Marilla Cuthbert certainly did. They balanced each other out. All parents are faced with the dilemma of how much control to give to their kids, and some feel very strongly about their personal philosophy. On one end of the spectrum are parents such as NC Wyeth who control everything their child does, says, eats, wears, and learns. On the other end would be parents such as radical unschoolers who don't believe in coercing their child to do anything.

Some of the eminent people I researched grew up with relatively little structure, but they wished they had had more. Dave Thomas, the founder of Wendy's restaurants, had a nomadic lifestyle with his father. They frequently moved as his father looked for work as a construction worker, living in rented rooms and eating at local diners. Dave's real sense of continuity and structure came from spending summers with his beloved grandmother.

Gloria Steinem was another child who lived a nomadic lifestyle with her restless father and unstable mother. Her parents did not coerce her to do anything, but after her mother left her father, Gloria soon learned to shoulder the responsibility of caring for herself and her invalid mother because there was no one else to do it. She did not have the freedom to pursue her own interests until her father agreed to take over care of her mother temporarily.

> *"One of the advantages of being disorderly is that one is constantly making exciting discoveries."*
>
> —A.A. Milne

Most of the people I researched grew up in households where there were rules, boundaries, and the expectation that the children would help with chores, or work to provide income for the family. The children were taught their parents' standards of morality, manners, and values. Many were purposely taught the life skills they would need as adults, including the basics of reading, writing, and arithmetic. But beyond that, most of these children were free to pursue their own learning. They chose their own books, devised their own experiments, drew whatever interested them, and built their own inventions.

Of the children who were forced to go to school for a period of time, the experience was almost always negative. C.S. Lewis was sent away to private schools when he was ten and he remembered them as brutal, demoralizing prison camps. "There was also a great decline in my imaginative life. For many years Joy (as I have defined it) was not only absent but forgotten."[15]

NC Wyeth chose to teach his children at home for the very reason that he wanted to preserve their individuality and creativity. The year Andrew was born, NC wrote:

> The sheeplike tendency of human society soon makes inroads on a child's *un*sophistications, and then popular education completes the dastardly work with its systematic formulas, and *away* goes the individual, hurtling through space into that hateful oblivion of mediocrity. We are pruned to stumps, one resembling the other, without character or grace.[16] [emphasis in the original]

As mentioned before, though, NC replaced conformity with his own enforced ideas of greatness. He was very controlling, although Andrew was lucky that by the time he was born, NC's fierce hold on the family had loosened. He describes himself then as "just wandering over the hills looking at things, not particularly thinking about art, just perfectly to myself. I developed sort of unconsciously on the outskirts of the family without too much scrutinizing. I think my father had had it watching the other children so much. When I came along he sort of said, 'Oh, shit. Let him grow.'"[17]

Play

Have you ever noticed how much of children's play is imitating the activities they see adults performing? Toy manufacturers know this. That is why we have toy kitchens, toy workbenches, toy lawn mowers, toy cars, toy make-up, and all the rest. Children, just like other young mammals, are driven to imitate their elders. Kittens stalk, puppies pounce, and children play house.

Maria Montessori found that when children were given the opportunity and real tools to perform meaningful work, their need to play-act disappeared. They were allowed to cut vegetables with real knives (not fake plastic vegetables with fake plastic knives). They were allowed to sweep with real brooms—cut shorter for their stature, but not toys. They gardened with quality tools, not fake ones.

Just think of how much is made or marketed for children that is fake or of inferior quality. Products are dressed up in bright eye-catching colors or adorned with popular media characters, but underneath is just another cheap temporary distraction that the child will soon grow bored with. This applies not just to toys, but to furnishings, art supplies, shoes, popular store-front books, school supplies, and food!

It is far better for children to have a few good toys rather than piles of cheap toys. Save the money spent on too much junk and apply it to just a few high quality things that the child can use again and again. Art and craft supplies marketed for children are typically low quality and frustrating to use. Invest in the real stuff. Good tools that are made to fit a child's size are very useful (with supervision)—brooms, rakes, shovels, carts, sharp scissors, hammers, saws, and the like. Some toys are completely open-ended, allowing for hours of satisfying play—blocks, construction sets, dolls, stuffed animals, sandboxes, balls, carts, etc. Sometimes the best toys of all are not even considered toys—empty boxes, scarves, sheets, stumps, and sticks all can be repurposed into forts, spaceships, castles, and costumes.

> *"You can do anything with children if you only play with them."*
>
> —Otto Von Bismarck

Fantasy

When observing that children did not seem to need pretend play when they were given the opportunity to do real work, Maria Montessori also discounted the need for fantasy play or fairy tales. The teachers in her classrooms did not even read stories to the children (although this practice may have changed in modern classrooms). Here is one area where Charlotte Mason did not agree with Ms. Montessori. Charlotte Mason did agree that young children learn well using their hands, but she believed "living books" formed the very life and soul of a proper education. This included fairy tales, folk tales, and other imaginative stories.

> *"Let early education be a sort of amusement, you will then better be able to find out the natural bent of the child."*
>
> —Plato

In addition to hearing stories, children love to act out the stories they have heard or imagined. Young C.S. Lewis relished the hours he spent with his older brother drawing and inventing their complex imaginary world of "Animal Land." Their world became more detailed as the boys grew older, complete with written histories, political intrigue, stories, and maps.

Young George Patton played rambunctious outdoor games at his family's California vineyard home. As might be expected, his favorite game was playing soldier with his sister Anne. Agatha Christie had a collection of imaginary friends, including a school of girls and a complicated assortment of make-believe kings and queens. Author Margaret Atwood played with marionettes and performed puppet shows with her friends.

Andrew Wyeth enjoyed toy soldiers and spent hours playing Robin Hood with friends in the nearby woods. His father's controlling tendencies, however, reached even into his play. Wyeth wrote: "Pa kept me almost in a jail, just kept me to himself in my own world, and he wouldn't let anybody in on it. I was almost *made* to stay in Sherwood Forest with Maid Marion and the rebels."[18] Andrew was forbidden to cross the road through town or have friends over to play (although he was allowed to play with other children in the woods).

Research on creativity has definitely shown that a playful, curious approach to problem solving inspires much more creative solutions. Einstein was one who was enamored with children's minds, how they think and see the world with unfiltered eyes. He wrote: "When I examine myself and my methods of thought I come to the conclusion that the gift of fantasy has meant more to me than my talent for absorbing positive knowledge."[19]

Pablo Picasso also respected the fresh perspective of children. "What one can consider an early genius is actually the genius of childhood." He believed that he lacked this genius because all his early work is too literal and precise. At an exhibition of children's work, he said, "When I was their age I could draw like Raphael, but it has taken me a whole lifetime to learn to draw like them."[20]

"The kernel of creativity," says psychologist Teresa Amabile, "is there in the infant: the desire and drive to explore, to find out about things, to try things out, to experiment with different ways of handling things and looking at things. As they grow older, children begin to create entire universes of reality in their play."[21]

> *"Childhood should be given its full measure of life's draught, for which it has an endless thirst."*
>
> —Rabindranath Tagore

The Stages of Creativity

You may already be familiar with Howard Gardner's theory of multiple intelligences. From his research he has identified seven different forms of intelligences that we all seem to have in varying amounts: linguistic, spatial, mathematical, kinesthetic, musical, artistic, interpersonal, intrapersonal, and naturalistic. He then studied famous examples of these highly creative intelligence types to see what conclusions he might infer.

He published the results of his research in a book called *Creating Minds: An Anatomy of Creativity Seen Through the Lives of Freud, Einstein, Picasso, Stravinsky, Eliot, Graham, and Gandhi.*

> *"The power of imagination makes us infinite."*
>
> —John Muir

One interesting thing he discovered was the pattern of developing individual creativity and how these people evolved to the height of their powers.

As children, these famous people were blessed with ample freedom and support from their parents to explore a variety of things, guided by their own interests. Gardner writes:

> The quality of these early years is crucial. If, in early life, children have the opportunity to discover much about their world and to do so in a comfortable, exploring way, they will accumulate invaluable 'capital of creativity,' on which they can draw in later life. If, on the other hand, children are restrained from such discovering activities, pushed in only one direction, or burdened with the view that there is only one correct answer or that correct answers must be meted out only by those in authority, then the chances that they will ever cast out on their own are significantly reduced.[22]

After a period of exploring, tinkering, and self-educating, the child (usually adolescent by this time) seems to outgrow the resources of her immediate family and begins to crave mentorship or a challenge to her growing abilities. Adolescents may still be interested in a variety of topics, but at some point (maybe not until they are adults) they discover a specific passion. Gardner adopts the term David Feldman coined "crystallizing experience" to describe this moment. After this crystallizing experience, it usually takes about ten years of study and practice for the individual to make her first creative breakthrough. To better describe these stages of creativity, I'll summarize the example Gardner developed for Albert Einstein.

Albert Einstein Through the Stages of Creativity

As a child in the exploring stage, Albert Einstein was very interested in objects, electric appliances, jigsaw puzzles, and objects with wheels and moving parts. He enjoyed building constructions of all sorts—he once built a giant house of cards fourteen stories high. He was not very verbal and did not do well in school. He particularly disliked the regimentation and rote learning required in German schools at the time. But he did enjoy learning on his own. When his Uncle Jakob introduced him to algebra and geometry he was hooked—fascinated by the beauty and order of mathematics.

As an adolescent, Einstein began to outgrow his own family's resources and become more focused in his scientific studies. A friend of the Einstein family and medical student, Max Talmey, helped by sharing his books with Albert. He provided classics such as the works of Kant and Darwin, as well as the latest books on physics. Einstein devoured everything he could of religion, philosophy, science, and mathematics. He also enjoyed mind puzzles—asking himself fanciful questions such as what it would be like for an observer to move alongside a light wave.

Although Einstein had better experiences later attending a progressive school with an emphasis on science, he continued his pattern of teaching himself outside of regular classes all the way through his years at the Zurich Polytechnic Institute. He was particularly interested in electromagnetism and the work of James Clark Maxwell, but the physics teacher at the Institute ignored these subjects. So Einstein cut classes and read the latest science publications for himself.

It was during these years at Zurich Polytechnic Institute that Einstein knew he wanted to explore the relations between electricity, magnetism, and the concepts of space, time, and ether. This was his "crystallizing ex-perience"—when he *knew* what he wanted to do. After graduation in 1901, Einstein could not get a job teaching so ended up working at a patent office in Bern, Switzerland. These were good years for him, though, because he met a number of scientifically minded friends and was able to work on physics in his free time (at the same time he got married and started a family).

> *"You can never solve a problem on the level on which it was created."*
>
> —Albert Einstein

He published a few average papers in those years, but his big breakthrough came in 1905 with the publication of four ma-jor papers—one of which was about his theory of relativity and another was the one that earned him a Nobel Prize seventeen years later. His scientific career took off, and by the 1920s he was known globally. So, it did not take Einstein a full ten years from the time he knew what he wanted to study to the publica-tion of his four great papers in 1905, but otherwise his creative evolution from childhood exploration ... to mentors ... to crys-tallizing experience ... to practice and mastery ... to creative breakthrough matches Howard Gardner's observations.[23]

Your Role in the Creative Process

Gardner admits that of course there are exceptions to this creative pattern, but it is nice to be aware of. In other words, don't be discouraged if your child's interest seems to jump from dinosaurs to aliens to magic to juggling without landing on any clear career path. The job of a child is to explore and learn. Your job is to support their learning without controlling it (other than obvious safety precautions).

Supporting your child's creative impulses is not laissez-faire parenting—it's hard work! Just think of how much time and effort Mrs. Spielberg devoted to cleaning cherry goop off the kitchen cabinets. It would have been easy for her to say "I'm too busy right now," or "Don't make a mess!" or "Can't you make a nice movie with no blood?" but she resisted the temptation, and now the rest of us benefit from watching his movies.

Remember This:

- Creativity is essential to fulfilling our life's purpose. It helps us survive, adapt, and evolve in new directions—the basis of civilization.
- Creativity thrives in freedom—freedom from control, freedom of choice, and free time.
- Children are already born creative. All we have to do is avoid squashing that creativity by controlling, evaluating, rewarding, or otherwise manipulating our kids. We also need to give them the time and freedom to play, help them when they want our help, and leave them alone when they don't.

Chapter Six
Passion Into Possibility

"A mentor is someone who allows you to see the hope inside yourself."
—Oprah Winfrey

Around the world, Albert Einstein's name has become synonymous with genius. No doubt he was brilliant, but he had help. His professors found him annoying, but there were other kindred spirits along the way who recognized his potential. There was the family friend and college student, Max Talmey, who lent young Albert books on science and philosophy. There was the beloved uncle, Caesar Koch, with whom he maintained a steady correspondence, sharing his ideas and writings. There was his Aunt Julie, who financially supported 17-year-old Einstein while he attended the Swiss Federal Polytechnical School in Zurich, a leading institution for science education. Einstein's best friend, Marcel Grossman, shared his notes for the classes Einstein missed and later helped teach him the necessary mathematical framework to present his general theory of relativity.

95

Those were just a few of Einstein's early friends and mentors; he had many more later in his professional life. One wonders how the course of Einstein's life and research might have been different without all those people. Would he have undertaken the same unconventional study of theoretical physics? Or would he have lived and died an unknown science professor, teaching the same material his professors tried to teach him? True mentors will slingshot a student farther than themselves, and farther even than the student dreams to go.

Every one of the people I studied had at least one mentor to help lead them on. Though a child's first mentors are within the family, as he or she grows older and discovers a particular passion, the youth needs to find someone more experienced in that field to guide and inspire. Whether it is science, business, dance, sports, or politics, mentors are living examples of what is possible. They are the instigators of achievement. I could cite a number of examples, but I'll focus on one.

Malcolm X

As you might imagine, civil rights activist Malcolm X had a difficult childhood. His parents were strong and well educated (his mother was raised on the British island of Grenada), but racial discrimination and the Great Depression challenged his family wherever they went. When they bought a house in a white neighborhood, the neighbors stoned and harassed them until finally their house was burned down in the middle of the night. The fire department refused to help them.

Things got even worse when Malcolm's father was killed (bashed on the head then laid across streetcar tracks to be cut in half), and his mother was left with seven small children to care for. But Malcolm was smart and did well in school. He got along well with his white classmates, and was even elected class president in the eighth grade. Unfortunately, this did not dissuade his favorite teacher from counseling him not to bother attending high school because he could not be hired to do any job requiring a high school education. When Malcolm told him he wanted to be a lawyer, the teacher seemed upset and said, "We all here like you, you know that. But you've got to be realistic about being a nigger. A lawyer—that's no realistic goal for a nigger. You need to think about something you can be. You're good with your hands. Why don't you plan on carpentry?"[1]

> Malcolm X
> 1925 - 1965
> *African American civil rights activist, leader within Nation of Islam organization*

It went downhill for Malcolm after that. He moved in with a sister in Boston and took odd jobs shining shoes and working as a clerk and busboy. Here he met other young black men who taught him how not to be "square," as they called it. He learned to speak like them and dress like them. Soon he moved to Harlem and immersed himself in the underground culture. Here he earned the nickname "Detroit Red" and began hustling the streets, selling marijuana, gambling, and running the numbers lottery for mobsters. He was not tough, but smart—and this was one of the few ways smart black men could make money.

After a while, he began using drugs and getting involved with gangs. At the age of 20 he was arrested for robbery and sentenced to 8 to 10 years of hard labor. This was a major turning point for Malcolm and he decided to use the time in prison to further his education.

He began reading a lot and applied for a transfer to an experimental prison in Norfolk with a large library. He took correspondence courses in Latin and English. He read biographies of Hannibal, Ibn Saud, Marx, Lenin, Stalin, Hitler, Rommel, Gandhi, Patrick Henry, and John Brown. He read

H.G. Wells and Will Durant, as well as volumes of black history and the philosophy of Plato, Aristotle, Spinoza, Nietzsche, and Schopenhauer. He also attended lectures offered by visiting scholars from Harvard and Yale.[2]

It was also at this library that he read about the other religions of the world, including Islam. Several of Malcolm's brothers and sisters had joined an organization called The Nation of Islam. This was a political as well as a religious organization. It differed from traditional Islam in that their goal was to form a separate black nation outside of the United States (or in some distinct part of the US). Jim Crow laws and lynchings were still disturbingly common. While other civil rights activists, such as Martin Luther King, Jr. advocated peaceful integration with white society, the Nation of Islam group did not believe such integration would ever be possible.

> *"My alma mater was books, a good library. I could spend the rest of my life reading, just satisfying my curiosity."*
> —Malcolm X

Malcolm was only mildly interested in this organization until he received a letter from the leader of the Nation of Islam, the Honorable Elijah Muhammed, who advised him not to consider himself a criminal. It was the whites and their unjust society who forced him to commit criminal acts—it was the whites who were to blame. The letter had such a powerful impact on Malcolm that he accepted the Nation of Islam's message and cause.

Elijah Muhammed became Malcom's mentor, as well as spiritual leader. When he was released from prison at the age of 27, Muhammed met him and challenged him not to return to vice and drugs. Malcolm became increasingly active in the Nation of Islam, recruiting, speaking, and later traveling to Africa and the Middle East speaking with heads of state. He devoted his life to Islam and fighting for the rights and dignity of blacks around the world.

Notice that in Malcolm's life he had a series of mentors that helped him through different stages of his development. Malcolm's first mentor, the eighth grade teacher, failed him. In his confusion and disillusionment, he found the young black men in Boston who were friendly, street-smart, and confident. Malcolm was impressed with the way they were unashamed to be black and wanted to be like them. Unfortunately those mentors could only help him up to a point before he started to get in trouble. It was his self-education and the powerful mentorship of the older Elijah Muhammed that marked the turning point in Malcolm's life. He ultimately outgrew Elijah Muhammed, becoming more famous and a mentor in his own right.

Unintentional Mentors

Sometimes people unintentionally become mentors simply by setting an example of what is possible. Writer Margaret Atwood grew up in the '50s when the feminist issue of career vs. family was becoming contentious. At the time, if women had jobs it was only to pass the time till they found a husband. It took guts to pursue a career. Fortunately, Margaret had a strong mother and aunts. Her mother's sisters were independent and supportive role models. One was already a writer who helped Margaret make the decision to disregard traditional gender roles. She decided at the age of 16 to become a writer.

Daniel Coyle, the author of *The Talent Code,* found that many great athletes come from communities where there was already a superstar example for the others to emulate. He gives the example of an unknown 19-year-old named Andruw Jones from the tiny Caribbean island of Curaçao. In the opening game of the 1996 World Series between the Atlanta Braves and the New York Yankees, rookie Jones shocked the baseball world with two consecutive home runs. A media storm of attention followed his debut, but it was nothing compared to the reaction in his hometown. Coyle writes:

> Curaçao's Little League founder, Frank Curiel, remembers the sound he heard when Jones hit the home runs. 'It was very, very loud. Firecrackers, yelling, everyone shouting, everyone waking up.' A few weeks later at Little League sign-ups the first aftershock showed up in the form of four hundred new kids. Their motivation was perhaps all the stronger since they knew that Jones hadn't even been one of the best players on the island. As a fifteen-year-old he had switched from third base to outfield so he could get more playing time.[3]

With Andruw Jones as an example of what could be accomplished, Curaçao boys have made it to the Little League World Series semifinals six times in the last eight years, winning the title in 2004 and placing second in 2005.

The intense desire to emulate can also inspire musicians. In *The Talent Code*, Coyle described a long-term study begun in 1997 by Gary McPherson to try to explain why some children make more musical progress than others. McPherson found that there was no real difference in aural sensitivity, motor skills, or sense of rhythm amongst the students he studied. The amount of time each child devoted to practice helped somewhat, but the children who progressed the most were the ones who had expressed a long-term commitment to play or who clearly knew that this is what they wanted to do. Something in their environment had ignited a passion to play, and with no more natural talent than anyone else, their performance jumped ahead.

McPherson gave one example of a girl named Clarissa who, despite all her teacher's efforts, showed lackluster results. The teacher had been trying to teach her a new song on her clarinet and Clarissa was not getting it. In desperation, he decided to play her a jazz version of the song. "When he played that, at that moment, something happened," McPherson explained. "Clarissa was awestruck by the jazz version. Entranced. She saw the teacher play it, and he must have played with some style, because she got an image of herself as a performer. The teacher didn't realize it then, but everything came together, and all of a sudden while hardly knowing it, she's on fire, desperate to learn."[4]

Daniel Coyle calls this phenomenon "ignition." He wrote, "What ignited the progress wasn't any innate skill or gene. It was a small, ephemeral, yet powerful idea: a vision of their ideal future selves, a vision that oriented, energized, and accelerated progress, and that originated in the outside world."[5] Something or someone from the child's environment triggers the inexplicable urge to pursue a certain path. This is the same "crystallizing moment" that psychologist Howard Gardner speaks of. It is not surprising that many musical youngsters come from families that are musical. The child grows up surrounded by people playing and enjoying music. For them, learning to play an instrument would be as natural as learning to read.

Intentional Mentors

Many children do not grow up in families that share their passions, and that is why it is so important for them to find outside mentors. Scientists, artists, statesmen, soldiers—all need mentors with the technical expertise to help them advance to the next level.

The inventor of the radio, Guglielmo Marconi, adored science and was forever duplicating experiments and building gadgets instead of doing schoolwork, much to his father's displeasure. But his mother arranged for him to have private science lessons and helped hide his contraptions from his father. Later, when he was not accepted into university, she searched out and found a local professor who agreed to mentor her son and let him use the university's laboratory and library. Marconi then continued his experiments while reading the work of other scientists and attending lectures.

Mentors can inspire and challenge a student because they are living proof of what is possible, and they know how to get there. It can be very difficult for a budding artist growing up in a community of engineers or for a budding engineer growing up in a community of artists to know what to do. They need people who share the same passions and speak the same language. J. Doyne Farmer, one of the pioneers of Chaos and Complexity theory, was always interested in science but grew up in the "sticks." He credits his success to a physicist friend who started as a Boy Scout leader but became his personal mentor (and eventually guardian) in physics, intellectual stimulation, new ideas, inventing/fixing things, as well as hiking and the outdoors.[6]

Even if students cannot find a live mentor, they can study the written works or masterpieces of past giants. Pablo Picasso's parents enrolled him in various formal art classes but he had no patience for the mediocre teachers, so he spent his time in galleries, studying great artists of the past. He eventually enrolled in the Academy of Fine Arts in Madrid but could not bear to stay there either because he felt that he was more competent than any of the instructors. So he continued his self-education, eventually traveling to Paris where he was exposed to the vital artists and movements of his day—impressionism, postimpressionism and expressionism.

> *"I've seen and met angels wearing the disguise of ordinary people living ordinary lives."*
>
> —Tracy Chapman

The role model could even be a celebrity or movie/television character that the child has never met. New York City Police Commissioner Bernard Kerik remembers being strongly influenced by the Green Hornet and Bruce Lee. He loved watching TV shows about cops and saw the movie *Serpico* with Al Pacino about 20 times. He was friendly with the cops he met in person and always stopped to watch them work. He admired the way cops actually did

> *"I've never been to New Zealand before. But one of my role models, Xena, the warrior princess, comes from there."*
>
> —Madeleine Albright

something to solve problems when it appeared that no one else did. Watching them, he could see himself making a difference, protecting people, and confronting injustice.

Finding Mentors

A child's education may begin at home, but at some point they need more than Mom and Dad can provide. They need to have fresh experiences, meet new people, and visit new places to help them discover what they like to do. And if they already know what they like, they need a more experienced mentor in that field to move them forward. Public school advocates may say that this is a good reason to send children off to school— to meet friends and broaden their horizons. Maybe; if there is simply no other way to meet people, school might be the best option. But this hardly seems necessary if a child has access to extended family, neighbors, religious congregations, homeschool groups, clubs, teams, or other community groups.

Take your kids to the library, museums, community events, concerts, summer programs, and club activities. Arrange field trips for your homeschool group. If you meet someone with an interesting skill such as glass blowing, dog training, or drumming, ask if they would be willing to hold a workshop for local students. Take advantage of nearby colleges and private schools if they have classes open to homeschooled students. There is no need to pressure a child to find her passion, just be on the look-out for opportunities she might enjoy. But if your student already knows what she wants to do, help her find her next teacher. It's easier these days to find opportunities because of the Internet and Yellow Pages. If your child really wants to fix guitars or learn welding or train for a triathlon, it is much easier now to find someone who can help.

Along these same lines, consider mentoring someone else's child or offering to lead a class for local homeschoolers. If you are an expert at robotics or fly-fishing but your own kids aren't interested, offer your help to other kids who would jump at the chance to learn. Many homeschooling parents form cooperative groups where one Spanish-speaking parent could teach Spanish, one nature-loving parent could lead nature walks, one tech-savvy parent could teach programming, and so on. If we hope for someone else to share their experience with our children, it's only fair to do the same for others. You never know what a difference you could make!

Remember This:

- Even the most brilliant and talented individuals need help.
- Mentors, whether intentional or unintentional, have a huge influence over us. Whatever our passion, mentors help us take it to the next level.
- Help your kids meet new interesting people, especially in their field of interest. Don't be bashful about looking for mentors!
- Consider mentoring someone yourself.

Part Two

Determination

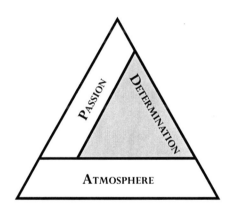

Chapter Seven
Attitude is Everything

"Nothing can stop the man with the right mental attitude from achieving his goal; nothing on earth can help the man with the wrong mental attitude."

—Thomas Jefferson

Young George Patton always knew he would be a great soldier. Steeped in the stories of Homer, Shakespeare, and Rudyard Kipling along with tales of his own Scotch and Confederate ancestors, he simply decided on a life of heroism. Struggles with reading, math, spelling, and other academic hurdles were just challenges to be conquered. He *craved* challenge—as a horseman, Olympic athlete, fencing champion, sailor, and soldier. Whatever people may have said about his faults, no one could deny his charisma. He had enough attitude to supply an army, literally.

Discovering one's passion is only half the battle. Without the courage and self-confidence to *act* on that passion, nothing will ever happen. Successful people are always trying to tell the rest of us to be bold, audacious—to just do it. They say there is nothing special about them, only that they took a chance and believed in themselves.

Success guru Napoleon Hill called it "Positive mental attitude." Norman Vincent Peale called it the "Power of Positive Thinking."

Orison Swett Marden, the founder of *Success* magazine, didn't just think of it as prerequisite to success. He called it the "Secret of Happiness" and "Heart Sunshine." He wrote:

> There is no other thing in human philosophy which pays so well, from every point of view, as the cultivation of heart sunshine, a cheerful outlook upon life, a mental attitude that sees the best instead of the worst side of everything. It is the most magical of physicians, for it heals all ills and affords a balm for all the sorrows and misfortunes of life.[1]

Patton was not exactly the "heart sunshine" type, but he had a true zest for life. Where does this come from? It is certainly possible for people to just teach themselves, as they grow older and wiser. But a lot of it can be learned in childhood, both by watching the adults around us, and more importantly, by the sure knowledge of being loved. George's parents adored him and he in turn adored them. He so revered his father that even as an adult, he would stand whenever his father entered the room.

George Patton
1885 - 1945
US Army officer, General during WWII

Every one of the successful people I researched had at least one strong parental figure in their lives—usually the mother, but sometimes it was the father or a grandparent or all of the above. Parents and other family members have a tremendous influence on how kids feel about themselves. There is nothing that can replace that feeling of being loved, just as we are.

Mothers

Thomas Edison was quick to credit his mother for his success. He told an interviewer, "I did not have my mother very long, but in that length of time she cast over me an influence which has lasted all my life... I was always a careless boy, and with a mother of different mental

> *"Attitude is more important than the past, than education, than money, than circumstances, than what people do or say. It is more important than appearance, giftedness, or skill."*
>
> —W.C. Fields

caliber I should have probably turned out badly. But her firmness, her sweetness, her goodness, were potent powers to keep me in the right path." He also said, "My mother was the making of me. She was so true, so sure of me; and I felt I had someone to live for, someone I must not disappoint."[2]

Napoleon Hill discovered through his "analysis of the work and achievements of hundreds of men of outstanding accomplishment, that there was the influence of a woman's love behind nearly *every one of them*." [emphasis orginal][3]

When success expert Orison Swett Marden asked the famous yacht builder, John B. Herreshoff, about his prime requirement for success, Herreshoff replied:

> I shall have to answer that by a somewhat humorous but very shrewd suggestion of another, —select a good mother. Especially for boys, I consider an intelligent, affectionate but considerate mother an almost indispensable requisite to the highest success. If you would improve the rising generation to the utmost, appeal first to the mothers.[4]

Herreshoff then advised Marden to teach mothers this:

> Above all things else, show them that reasonable self-denial is a thousandfold better for a boy than to

109

have his every wish gratified. Teach them to encourage industry, economy, concentration of attention and purpose, and indomitable persistence.[5]

He believed that mothers often tried to do this but ended up indulging their children more than they should.

So what were the mothers of famous homeschoolers like? Strict? Indulgent? Or some combination of both? I did not find a single mother whom I would classify as indulgent (overly permissive, gift giving), but I found a few who were overly controlling.

General Douglas MacArthur's mother was quite strict about manners, protocol, and appearance; but she allowed her young boys—shirtless with headbands and fringed hide leggings—to ride ponies and shoot rabbits in the rugged southwest army fort home of their childhood. Her highest ideals were courage, patriotism, and honesty. She insisted on her children saluting for every flag raising or lowering, or for any adult visiting, or even for patriotic stories in the newspaper. She read them stories of heroism. She would not allow them to cry, and tucked them in with the words, "You must grow up to be a great man like your father."[6] She even followed Douglas to West Point, renting quarters nearby the military reservation so that she could keep a close eye on his progress.

> "My mother was the most beautiful woman I ever saw. All I am I owe to my mother. I attribute all my success in life to the moral, intellectual and physical education I received from her."
>
> —George Washington

Frank Lloyd Wright and Franklin Delano Roosevelt also had domineering mothers, who followed their grown sons from house to house interfering with their careers and relationships. These sons tend to form mutually dependant relationships with such mothers. They resent their mothers' demands, but at the same time, cannot bear to be apart from them.

Interestingly, the authors of *Cradles of Eminence* found that domineering/smothering mothers were not at all unusual among famous people. Perhaps it is a mother's force of will that propels her offspring to success, or perhaps her absolute conviction in the superiority of her own child (very often at the expense of her other children). The authors found

> *"One good mother is worth a hundred schoolmasters."*
>
> —George Herbert

that many of the dictators, military leaders, and adventurers from their list of 700 subjects had smothering mothers—Adolph Hitler, Joseph Stalin, Benito Mussolini, Friedrich Nietzsche, among others.

The bulk of mothers I studied however, matched the description of Herreshoff's ideal mother. They were supportive yet allowed their children to make mistakes. They were interested in their children's accomplishments, but had interests of their own to occupy their time. They were conscientious, responsible, good listeners, and generally cheerful. Intelligent, even if not well educated, most of the mothers had strong convictions about morals and health related issues.

Author Margaret Atwood was impressed that her mother was not like other mothers of the 1950s. Living in the backwoods of Canada, her mother was brave and practical, raising two children alone for long periods of time while their zoologist father was occupied with forest research. She once chased off a bear, could use a gun and bow and arrow, fished regularly, and took up ice-skating at the age of 46.

Many mothers were described as imaginative and good at telling stories. Agatha Christie's mother was very playful and interested in the supernatural. John Muir's mother, though suffering under her husband's thumb, escaped for long walks in the woods with her children. She secretly enjoyed drawing, painting, writing poetry, and embroidery.

111

Fathers

Not everyone I studied had a strong mother, but in those cases the child was fortunate to have a terrific father or grandparent to take her place. Photographer Ansel Adam's mother was chronically depressed, needy, and unsupportive of her husband. Adams rarely mentioned her but was devoted to his courageous, long-suffering father. In his autobiography he wrote:

> I often wonder at the strength and courage my father had in taking me out of the traditional school situation and providing me with these extraordinary learning experiences. I am certain he established the positive direction of my life that otherwise, given my native hyperactivity, could have been confused and catastrophic. I trace who I am and the direction of my development to those years of growing up in our house on the dunes, propelled especially by an internal spark tenderly kept alive and glowing by my father.[7]

Another example of a great father was Theodore Roosevelt, Sr., christened "Greatheart" by his children. He was a wealthy philanthropist, always busy with various social causes, but he showed great care and interest in his children. Teddy Roosevelt described him thus in his autobiography:

> My father, Theodore Roosevelt, was the best man I ever knew. He combined strength and courage with gentleness, tenderness, and great unselfishness. He would not tolerate in us children selfishness or cruelty, idleness, cowardice, or untruthfulness. As we grew older he made us understand that the same standard of clean living was demanded for the boys as for the girls; that what was wrong in a woman could not be

right in a man. With great love and patience, and the most understanding sympathy and consideration, he combined insistence on discipline. He never physically punished me but once, but he was the only man of whom I was ever really afraid. I do not mean that it was a wrong fear, for he was entirely just, and we children adored him.[8]

Teddy Roosevelt's mother, on the other hand, was childish and ineffectual as a mother figure. She was a beautiful, vivacious southern belle with a knack for telling stories and a sense of humor. But she thought Teddy was an ugly child and nothing he did could ever quite please her. He never openly disobeyed her because his beloved father would not stand for it, but he was condescending in his own way, answering her requests with, "Oh, yes, you pretty sweet thing."[9]

Grandparents

In some cases, it was a grandmother or other parent figure who had the greatest influence on a child. Dave Thomas, the founder of Wendy's restaurants, was only five when his mother died, and he lived a nomadic lifestyle with his quiet father. But every summer, he went to live with his grandmother. "The days I spent with my Grandmother Minnie Sinclair were the best times of my childhood, and she was the greatest influence in my young life. She knew what she wanted and went after it. She always had time for me, and when I did something right, she made me feel 10 feet tall and very, very special. The greatest lesson she taught me: Don't cut corners on quality."[10]

Though archeologist Margaret Mead had both a strong mother and a strong father, she credits her grandmother as the greatest influence in her life. Her college educated grandmother believed that every child had the right to grow up on a farm, so

Margaret and her siblings spent more time learning about chickens, cooking, plants, animals, and household chores than they did academic work. Margaret wrote: "The result was that I was not well drilled in geography or spelling. But I learned to observe the world around me and to note what I saw—to observe flowers and children and baby chicks. She taught me to read for the sense of what I read and to enjoy learning."[11]

When Unconditional Love is Missing

Whether it's a mother, father, grandparent, or some other surrogate parent figure, every child needs someone to love them and believe in their abilities. One of the more interesting stories I found about Thomas Edison was not about his childhood, but about his fatherhood. He may have been a great inventor but he was a lousy father.

Edison had two sets of three children with his first and second wives. His first wife, Mary, was very young when they married and had chronic health problems. She was very submissive and usually stayed at home alone with the children while Edison was forever working. He had an extreme work ethic, and often slept under his workbench rather than go home. Mary died, probably of a brain tumor, after thirteen years of marriage.

Two years later, Edison married Mina, who was older, stronger, and better educated than Mary had been. His children from the first marriage, Marion, Thomas Jr., and William, were welcomed by their stepmother but sent away to school or Europe by their father. As a result they always felt as if they had been shoved aside to make room for the new babies.

Tom Jr. wrote home from prep school in 10th grade:

> Dear Papa . . . I worry so I cannot study at all which knocks me all out of sorts. . . If I could only study at home I can look forward to unlimited time, I mean I

114

will study as hard as I possibly could, because it is for my own benifit [sic] that I should do so, because *then* I could get through a great deal quicker, *which I know is exactly what you want me to do, is it not?* . . Write as soon as you possibly can papa will you please. *I feel badly.*[12] [italics in original]

The second son William Leslie wrote home:

"I realy [sic] cannot stand it up here. I do not like the masters and they don't like me. I cannot study because I am so unhappy . . . May I come home and go to a public school or any school near home. If you want to put me out of Misery you will say yes if you don't you will say no."[13]

Edison did not have much more time to spend with his three younger children, Madeleine, Charles, and Theodore. While they were little he spent most of his time at the Ogden Mines. Madeleine remembers visiting the mines at the age of six: "We went up there once. We drove up. It took us two days to get there. That was the first time I think I realized I had a father. He used to be away all week except Saturday when he'd come back. He was just a 'presence' to me."[14]

Although Edison was still largely absent from the lives of his second set of children, these children were fortunate to have a strong mother to care for them. She was a fan of the Montessori method and very conscientious with their upbringing. She read classics such as Shakespeare, Tennyson, Charles Lamb, and the Old Testament to the children for an hour before dinner believing it was good for their moral development.

By the time the children were old enough to attend school, Edison was finished with the mines and able to spend more time with his family. He was always trying to teach them a lesson of some kind. At breakfast, he would quiz them on their previous day's homework and vocabulary checklists maintained by their mother. He also enlisted their help in searching through scientific reference books for citations to help him with his laboratory work. On Sunday afternoon nature walks, Edison would challenge his children to find varieties of every form of vegetation they could find, then match their cuttings with his at the end of the walk to find out who had the most. Edison usually won.[15]

The end result of these two types of parenting styles couldn't be more different. His three older children were very unhappy and unsuccessful. Marion went away to Europe when she felt that she had been replaced in her father's affections and the two never reconciled.

Tom Jr., a sensitive artistic type, failed at nearly everything he tried to do. Following is an excerpt from one of his many letters to his stepmother Mina:

> I often wonder – and think – am I his son . . . what have I done? to be deserving of such – a great and honorable Father . . . and it is his genius – I have to blame for these doubtful and restless thoughts of mine . . . I probably never will be able to please him – I have no genius – no talent and no accomplishment – I am afraid – it is not in me – but I shall never give up trying – if I could only talk to him the way I want to – I have many ideas of my own – which sometimes . . . I would like to ask him – or tell him about – but they never leave my mouth.[16]

Younger brother William Leslie did even worse than his brother at school, but when the headmaster tried to have a conference with Thomas Edison, he received no reply and was told by William that all such matters would have to be handled by Mrs. Edison. Will became very wasteful, spending money

116

quickly, borrowing money on his father's good name until creditors started approaching Edison to collect. Both boys tried to start businesses using their Edison name to lure customers, but neither was successful. After further embarrassments, Thomas finally paid off his son Tom Jr. to change his name.

The three younger children fared much better. Madeleine was more of a social butterfly than a scholar and eventually disappointed her parents when she married a Catholic aviator. But she had four children (the only grandchildren Edison would have) and later became involved with politics, reform, and administering her father's birthplace museum after her mother's death. Charles became a very sensible, valuable manager in his father's business and later moved into politics as Assistant Secretary of the Navy and Governor of New Jersey. Theodore graduated from MIT, later returning there for postgraduate work in engineering, biology, and geology. He started his own invention company and used his great wealth for environmental and pacifist causes.

> *"Neither a lofty degree of intelligence nor imagination nor both together go to the making of genius. Love, love, love, that is the soul of genius."*
>
> — Wolfgang Amadeus Mozart

We will never know all the details of how these children were raised or what kind of mother Mary was, but it certainly seems that Mina's children had better self-esteem and confidence than Miriam, Tom Jr., and William. Mina tried to help her stepchildren, but they couldn't shake the feeling of being rejected by their famous father. Charles knew enough to give credit to his mother and told her, "If not for your teaching and letters, I would have followed Tom and William as naturally as going to sleep."[17]

You're Being Watched

Aside from offering unconditional love and support, the

117

best thing we can do for our kids is model a positive attitude. They're watching you all the time, good or bad, so you might as well make it good. They take their cues from you. Have you ever noticed your child using a particular expression or mannerism over and over and wonder where it came from? Check the mirror! Whether it's charming or just embarrassing, you may not even realize that you huff or roll your eyes until you catch your sweet little daughter doing the same thing. Kids learn more from watching and listening to you than you may realize. They notice how you react to things, how fast you give up, how hard you work. They notice the smile on your face. And they especially notice laughter. Are you judgmental or forgiving? Do you complain about people or praise people behind their backs? Do you take notice of and appreciate the little things in life? Do you find yourself saying "No" more often than "Yes?"

I don't mean that you should be perpetually giddy with optimism and forced cheerfulness, but make a conscious decision to reject negative reactions. You may have unconsciously picked up these thought patterns from your own parents or peers. But no worries—thoughts can be changed. If you recognize the signs of negativity in yourself, please consider an attitude overhaul. It will be so helpful for everything you do now and in the future.

It's Never Too Late to Learn

> *"Most folks are as happy as they make up their minds to be."*
> —Abraham Lincoln

Some people seem blessed with a naturally cheerful disposition, but in the absence of mental illness, it is possible for everyone to develop a positive mental attitude. The gurus advise us that we all have the power to make ourselves miserable or happy depending on our thoughts. We choose how we think. We can decide to think helpful, hopeful, cheerful thoughts—even if it seems forced and artificial at first. With enough practice, the habit will take hold.

Success expert Orison Swett Marden gave this advice for practicing self-control:

> If your great weakness is to storm and rage on the slightest provocation, if you 'fly all to pieces' over the least annoyance, do not waste your time regretting this weakness, and telling everybody that you cannot help it. Take exactly the opposite course. Do not speak of your failing at all. Follow Shakespeare's injunction and 'assume a virtue if you have it not.' Deliberately, continually assume the calm, balanced composure which characterizes your ideal person. Try to persuade yourself by the constant, quiet, but firm assurance that instead of being hot-tempered, nervous, or excitable, you are really calm, serene, and well balanced, that you do not fly off at a tangent at every little annoyance, but that you can control yourself perfectly. In a little while you will be surprised to find how the perpetual holding of this attitude will mold you to your thought, will help you to grow into the very image of your state of mind. All we are, or have been, or ever will be, comes from the quality and force of our thinking.[18]

And though changing your thoughts sounds simple enough, it can be hard to do without someone to talk you through it. One very helpful book I would recommend is: *Happy for No Reason: 7 Steps to Being Happy from the Inside Out* by Marci Shimoff. This book will change your life—and make you a better parent, not because of any specific parenting tips but because you will be a stronger, more emotionally healthy person.

Remember This:

- Success starts with a positive attitude.
- A positive attitude starts with love. Every child needs at least one person who loves him or her completely, but more is even better.
- Mothers, fathers, stepparents, grandparents, aunts, uncles, siblings, cousins, and friends are all wonderful if they are available.
- Nothing can replace that implicit awareness of being loved, just as we are. And a child who has been denied that will often spend the rest of his life trying to fill that hole. Loving a child just as he is means that you will not try to change him or make him more like you—you love him just the way he is, faults and all.
- We are always modeling attitude, whether we realize it or not. Children learn by example.
- No matter what our physical circumstances, we choose how to respond. We are not responsible for our child's happiness, but we can show them how to be happy by taking responsibility for own thoughts.

Chapter Eight
Clear Grit

"Talent is cheaper than table salt. What separates the talented individual from the successful one is a lot of hard work."

—Stephen King

Much has been said in contemporary media recently of the "Law of Attraction," particularly as presented by Rhonda Byrne in *The Secret*. The theory alleges that what we think about and believe, good or bad, will become truth. Proponents claim that to achieve our dreams, all we must do is decide what we want, send out a request to the universe, then believe and behave as if the request will be fulfilled.

The difference here between the modern "Law of Attraction" and the older "Think and Grow Rich" philosophy of success guru Napoleon Hill, is that desire and belief, while extremely important, are only the beginning of success. Hill went on to identify other vitally important steps to success such as: specialized knowledge, imagination, organized planning, decision, and persistence. The eminent people he and Orison Swett Marden interviewed did not achieve greatness merely by thinking about it—they *worked* at it.

> *"Young people continually prate of genius. They seem to think that every person who does a great thing in the world must be a genius, a man with superb talent, but, as a matter of fact, the greater number of men who have made history were men of ordinary talents, but with very extraordinary application, great industry, men with common ability, but with mighty uncommon persistence, determination and clear grit."* [1]
>
> —Orison Swett Marden

Thomas Edison is a famous example of persistence. The man used to work up to twenty hours a day in a lab, before he relaxed his schedule to only fourteen hours a day. Following is an excerpt from Orison Swett Marden's interview with Thomas Edison:

"'You lay down rather severe rules for one who wishes to succeed in life,' I ventured, 'working eighteen hours a day.'"

'Not at all,' he said. 'You do something all day long, don't you? Every one does. If you get up at seven o'clock and go to bed at eleven, you have put in sixteen good hours, and it is certain with most men, that they have been doing something all the time. They have been either walking, or reading, or writing, or thinking. The only trouble is that they do it about a great many things and I do it about one. If they took the time in question and applied it in one direction, to one object, they would succeed. Success is sure to follow such application. The trouble lies in the fact that people do not have an object—one thing to which they stick, letting all else go. Success is the product of the severest kind of mental and physical application.' [2]

Andrew Carnegie

Another self-taught entrepreneur, Andrew Carnegie was a firm believer in doing every job to the best of his abilities. His destitute family immigrated to the United States from Scotland when Andrew was twelve. His mother found odd jobs repairing shoes but his father was unable to find work as a weaver, and could not learn or tolerate any new occupation.

At age thirteen, Carnegie got a job as a bobbin boy at the nearby Anchor Cotton Mill working a grueling twelve hours a day. He was happy for the work, though, and put his heart into it. Soon a visiting Scottish businessman noticed the plucky lad and offered him a job at twice the pay in his bobbin factory. His job was to feed the boiler and tend the engine that turned the lathes in the workshop. The boss soon discovered that Carnegie was good with arithmetic and so entrusted him with the book-keeping and a new nasty job of coating the newly turned bobbins with petroleum.

But, less than a year later, he was offered another opportunity through his uncle's connections to work as a messenger for the Pittsburgh office of the Atlantic & Ohio Telegraph Company. Carnegie offered to begin at once, and was determined to be the best messenger boy he could be. He worked hard to Americanize his accent, and learn his way around the crazy streets of Pittsburgh. "So I started in and learned all the addresses by heart, up one side of Wood Street and down the other. Then I learned the other business streets in the same way."[3] He memorized the names and faces of the local businessmen so that he could greet them and deliver messages should he see them on the street.

> Andrew Carnegie
> 1835 - 1919
> *Steel magnate, philanthropist*

Because of his manners and trustworthiness, his boss sometimes asked him to watch the office, to the disapproval of his peers. The other boys thought him a prig because he did not enjoy roughhousing or sexual banter. But Carnegie only wanted to improve himself, and his new goal was to become a telegraph operator. He tried to teach himself by listening and going to the office early, but finally convinced someone else to teach him. One morning, before the office was opened, an urgent message came in and instead of ignoring it, Carnegie took the message, translated it, and delivered it. He was afraid of being reprimanded, but his boss instead commended him. He began filling in when the regular operator was absent. He even taught himself to take the messages by ear instead of transcribing the printed slips as everyone else did.

> *"I don't wait for moods. You accomplish nothing if you do that. Your mind must know it has got to get down to work."*
> —Pearl Buck

Carnegie's plan for self-improvement—learning everything he could and doing every job to the best of his ability—led to more opportunities, more notice, and more connections. By the age of twenty-six, he was a very wealthy man, and since most of his income came from investments, he frequently took time off to travel, improve his education, and pursue interests such as fishing. The only reason he continued to work was because he couldn't resist the opportunities that were always available. He also decided how much money he really needed and gave the rest away as it came to him.

If you find it hard to imagine your son or daughter rising to the heights of such industry, do not despair. In reviewing the childhoods of famous people, I found that most children worked hardest for employers outside the family (the exception would be poor John Muir who worked under constant threat of a thrashing from his father). Perhaps it is the natural desire to please and impress someone new. This is not always the case of course; anyone who has had occasion to hire a youth (or adult) for a job knows that some are better workers than others.

Nurturing Willpower

So how does one youth become a cheerful, honest, diligent worker on his way to success and another remain sullen, lazy, incompetent, and useless? The difference is willpower. One youth has learned to choose what he will do, think, and say while the other only follows his impulses or the dictates of society. Even people who appear to be industrious, dress fashionably, and speak confidently have no real willpower if they are merely imitating society. They are putting on a show and probably don't even realize it.

How, you wonder, do we help our children develop willpower? Once again, modeling is the first step. Just as children learn about positive attitude by watching adults, they also learn about willpower. It is doubly hard for a child to develop self-control if the adults in their life don't have it, or the adults they see on TV don't have it. How could they know what is possible or what self-control means if they never even *see* it?

It doesn't have to be the parents. Sometimes other mentors can demonstrate what it means to show up, do your best, and follow through. In Carnegie's case it was his mother who showed him. He recognized his mother's hard work and later wrote of her: "We were not, however, reduced to anything like poverty compared with many of our neighbors. I do not know to what lengths of privation my mother would not have gone that she might see her two boys wearing large white collars, and trimly dressed."[4]

As long as someone can demonstrate a positive work ethic, it may not matter if the child also has negative examples (maybe that even helps!). Reformer and *New York Times* owner Horace Greeley grew up in dire poverty. His father was a drunk and couldn't hold a job but his mother managed to work enough for both of them, all while dedicating herself to those less fortunate. Horace followed her lead, refusing to drink or smoke the rest of his life and working tirelessly for social reform.

Tough Times

Some unfortunate children are forced to learn self-control as a matter of survival. Because of loss or hardship, they assumed tremendous responsibility at a young age—far more than modern youth are likely to experience.

Eli Whitney, the inventor of the cotton gin, was the oldest of four children when his mother became bedridden. At the tender age of five, Eli began caring for his siblings and the house with only the help of a nasty-tempered hired girl.

From the age of eleven his daily chore was to feed and water sixty head of cattle before walking to school. He also had his own business making nails, for nails were in short supply during the Revolutionary War. In his early teens, he took it upon himself to search out and hire a man to help him with the work (without asking permission of his father, though he was gone for three days). His sister Elizabeth later wrote, "He was remarkable for thinking and acting for himself at the age of ten or twelve years."[5]

Eli Whitney learned to think and act for himself because he was forced to—he had no one else to do it for him. His father had to stay in the fields all day, his mother was sick, and his baby brothers and sister needed help.

Composer Irving Berlin hit the streets at age fourteen to avoid burdening his family. Andrew Carnegie began working at the age of twelve. Walt Whitman quit school at the age of eleven to work as an office boy in an attorney's office.

Times were different then, of course. No one would expect

(or allow) a child to support his family today. But our children have lost a sense of importance and value because of it. Doing chores for pocket change or mowing lawns to save up for a video game just doesn't have the same panache as saving your family from starvation. We still live in an imperfect world though, and our kids still have a very good chance of encountering adversity. Teach them not to run or hide from it, but to conquer it.

Ambition

Sometimes self-control emerges from sheer ambition. Thomas Edison seems to have been extraordinarily—even obsessively—ambitious. He had perfectly nice, hard-working parents, but they were not the models for his intense work ethic. Maybe it was his personality or insatiable curiosity that drove him on.

General George Patton was another ambitious boy, but rather than curiosity, he was inspired by heroism. He had a fairly idyllic childhood growing up in his family's vineyard with devoted parents. His father read heroic novels to him and stories of great military leaders such as Hannibal, Caesar, Joan of Arc, Napoleon Bonaparte, Robert E. Lee, and Stonewall Jackson. George also craved romantic stories of his own Scotch and Confederate ancestors and was determined to live up to the family's honor. He spent his days riding horses, building forts, and playing soldier. Everything he did was driven by ambition—not just to be a soldier, but to be the *best* soldier.

> "*The reward of a thing well done, is to have done it.*"
>
> —Ralph Waldo Emerson

Even if a child learns self-discipline through adversity or ambition, they still need examples of what hard work looks like. So just as developing a positive mental attitude makes us better parents, developing our own willpower and ability to do the disagreeable makes us better role models. But there are other things

127

we can do to actively teach our kids to control themselves.

Practicing Willpower

Charlotte Mason, the famous Victorian era homeschool champion, had a lot to say about willpower. She considered it a fundamental aspect of education and warned that there are two great mistakes parents often make. One is to confuse "willful" behavior with force of will. If a toddler screams for candy or dominates his playmates, the parent excuses it with, "He has such a strong will," when in reality the child is only following his impulses. The other mistake is thinking that the child's will must be broken at all costs, leading to a life of punishment and repression.

The sensible route is between these two extremes. Her solution for harnessing the will, in children or adults, is deceptively simple. She explains:

> A little bit of nursery experience will show better than much talking what is possible to the will. A baby falls, gets a bad bump, and cries piteously. The experienced nurse does not 'kiss the place to make it well,' or show any pity for the child's trouble—that would make matters worse; the more she pities, the more he sobs. She hastens to 'change his thoughts,' so she says; she carries him to the window to see the horses, gives him his pet picture-book, his dearest toy, and the child pulls himself up in the middle of a sob, though he is really badly hurt. Now this, of the knowing nurse, is precisely the part the will plays towards the man. It is by force of will that a man can 'change his thoughts,' transfer his attention from one subject of thought to another, and that, with a shock of mental force of which he is distinctly con-

Charlotte Mason

If you have never heard of this Victorian era educator (and home school champion), I highly recommend reading some of the books by and about her. Charlotte Mason wrote her six-volume series on education at the turn of the century, a time when England was preoccupied with educational reform. The books sold well and soon after, the Parents National Education Union (PNEU) was established. Branches were set up in major cities and towns and the organization developed a monthly magazine, *The Parents Review*, edited by Charlotte Mason. She later opened a school for teachers and a correspondence school for parents and governesses teaching children at home.

scious. And this is enough to save a man and to make a man, this power of making himself think only of those things which he has beforehand decided that it is good to think upon.[6]

Charlotte Mason is not advocating *rewarding* a child to stop his crying. The object is to divert his attention to something else. When the child is older, Mason suggests reading biographies and stories that exemplify willpower, and discussing strategies for changing their thoughts when necessary.

Then, as was said before, let him know the secret of *willing*; let him know that, by an effort of will, he *can* turn his thoughts to the thing he wants to think of—his lessons, his prayers, his work, and away from the things he should not think of; —that, in fact, he can be such a brave, strong little fellow, he can *make* himself think of what he likes; and let him try little experiments—that if he once get his *thoughts* right, the rest will take care of itself, he will be sure to *do* right then; that if he feels cross, naughty thoughts coming upon him, the plan is, to think hard about something else, something nice—his next birthday, what he means to do when he is a man. Not all this at once, of course; but line upon line, precept upon precept, here a little and there a little, as opportunity offers. Let him get into the *habit* of managing himself, controlling himself, and it is astonishing how much self-compelling power quite a young child will exhibit.[7] [italics in original]

There is the risk here of merely training a child to "will" what we will for them. There are so many parents who, perhaps unconsciously, try to control everything their child does, says, eats, reads, or thinks. This leaves very little opportunity for the child to actually manage himself. Exercise of the will is really about making choices—good or bad. Children should be given the right to make choices and do for themselves as much as possible.

Another famous educator familiar to most homeschooling parents is Maria Montessori. She gave us this analogy for developing willpower:

> It would certainly never occur to any one that in order to educate the voluntary motility of a child, it would be well first of all to keep it absolutely motionless, covering its limbs with cement (I will not say fracturing them!) until the muscles become atrophied and almost paralyzed; and then, when this result had been attained, that it would suffice to read to the child wonderful stories of clowns, acrobats and champion boxers and wrestlers, to fire him by such examples, and to inspire in him an ardent desire to emulate them. It is obvious that such a proceeding would be an inconceivable absurdity.
>
> And yet we do something of the same kind when, in order to educate the child's 'will,' we first of all at-

tempt to annihilate it, or, as we say, 'break' it, and thus
hamper the development of every factor of the will,
substituting ourselves for the child in everything. It
is by *our* will that we keep him motionless, or make
him act; it is we who choose and decide for him. And
after all this we are content to teach him that 'to will
is to do' (*voler e potere*). And we present to his fancy,
in the guise of fabulous tales, stories of heroic men,
giants of will, under the illusion that by committing
their deeds to memory a vigorous feeling of emula-
tion will be aroused and will complete the miracle.[8]

Children will not be able to demonstrate self-mastery all at
once. Be patient with them! They will still make mistakes and
act "childish" or "willful" at times, but we should think of it as
practice. Just as an athlete must practice a move over and over
to get it right, we all (grown-ups included) must practice good
habits over and over to get them right.

The habit of self-mastery can be developed. Activities that
are important to the child such as sports, martial arts, music, art,
4H, Scouts, and other outdoor pursuits all offer the opportunity
for a child to experience responsibility, diligence, failure, and success—but not if the parent is running the show. If Mom always
packs the ballet bag or pesters her son to work on the next merit
badge, then the child doesn't "own" it—Mom does.

A cheerleading coach once told me that she had to forbid
mothers from bringing missing items to practice. If a girl forgot
her mandatory water bottle, it was common for the girl to simply
call her mother on the cell phone and Mom would drive back to
bring her one. The only consequence for the girl's mistake was
to have Mom fix it. Once the coach outlawed fetch and retrieve
habits, the girls were forced to sit on the sidelines throughout

practice—and they remembered to bring their water bottles next time.

Work Ethic

I've been using the terms work ethic, self-discipline, will-power, and self-control interchangeably because they are all so closely related. We use self-discipline to control our tempers, our habits, and our ability to do the disagreeable. Some work is fun for its own sake, but there will always be chores we'd rather not do or just get tired of. It takes a well-developed sense of discipline, or work ethic, to clean out the rain gutters or take care of deskwork when we'd rather be doing something else.

> *"Opportunity is missed by most people because it is dressed in overalls and looks like work."*
>
> —Thomas A. Edison

Some things take a long time to finish and it is worthwhile to keep working at it and experience the satisfaction of completion. If you are restoring an old car or building a rock wall or some other big project, work at it a little every day and you will automatically be teaching your children how to manage their own projects.

Determination to succeed or positive thinking does us little good if we're not willing to work for it. We can help our kids succeed by first modeling a responsible work ethic and then giving them an opportunity to practice it.

Try to do chores alongside your child, making it a friendly time for telling stories and chatting. Avoid too much instruction, just pitch in and let them watch you. By all means, encourage little ones to join you while you're folding laundry, pulling weeds, cooking dinner, etc. Smile. Listen to them. Don't worry if they are folding the clothes wrong or dripping mop water on the floor. They will get better by watching you—maybe even asking you to show them how to fold the shirts. The important thing is that you are showing them the work that must be done and that it can be done cheerfully.

It can be very frustrating for perfectionist parents to watch their child doing a job all wrong (or not the way they think it should be done), but it will take them time. Fine motor skills, attention span, and experience all need to come together before children can do the job as well as an adult. It would be worse for parents to rush perfection by lecturing ("No, no. I've told you this a hundred times"), demonstrating ("Here, let me show you"), and criticizing ("This is too sloppy!"). These are guaranteed to squash motivation.

Hold high standards for your own work and keep a positive attitude. Children will eventually notice how you do things, or even ask. Young children are wired to emulate and they naturally like to be around their parents. All you need to do is be your best self. Don't expect them to do everything just like you, because they are not you; but they will learn quite a bit.

If you are able to start this when your children are young and eager to tag along next to you, they will probably know how to do most household chores on their own by the time they are teenagers. Part of this process is not doing things for your children that they are capable of doing for themselves. If they are tall enough to reach into the washing machine, then they should be able to manage their own laundry. If they are able to prepare breakfast for themselves, maybe they could also prepare it for the whole family. If you have been cleaning their room alongside them long enough to show how it is done, at some point you need to turn responsibility for the room over to them to clean as they will (or won't).

"How do you eat an elephant? One bite at a time."

—Unknown

If you have a teen who is allergic to work, it might be better to foist them off on someone else. What I mean by this is the old-fashioned mentoring/apprentice system. Nearly all of the young people I studied were inclined to work harder for pay or job satisfaction outside the home than they were in doing chores inside the home (even for pay). This doesn't mean they were ungrateful. Indeed, many of those kids were happy to share their wages with the family. I think it's natural for teens to crave fresh experiences, greater responsibilities, and new mentors. Help your teens find a suitable job or volunteer opportunity.

Remember This:

- Success doesn't just happen—it takes work.
- Adversity and ambition can promote willpower, but it is also possible to train the will a little at a time. In order to train it, the child must be allowed to use it, and experience the natural consequences, good or bad.
- Controlling our behavior starts with controlling our thoughts.
- Just like a positive attitude, self-discipline is learned best by watching someone else, then practicing. As parents, we need to be aware of the example we are setting.
- Let kids work—don't do everything for them. They are far more capable than you may think. And when they are old enough, encourage them to find work opportunities outside the home.
- Patience, patience, patience! Self-discipline takes time.

Chapter Nine
Get Out of the Way

"You don't have to be great to start, but you have to start to be great."

—Zig Ziglar

One of the most important themes in success handbooks is setting a goal—a big, very specific goal. While this might be true for adults, I did not find much evidence of this among children who grew up to accomplish great things. They followed their interests, not knowing where they might lead but happy to immerse themselves. Beatrix Potter filled countless sketchbooks; little Louis Armstrong shadowed musicians; Orville and Wilbur Wright tinkered with lathes, machines, and toy "helicopters"; young Robert Frost devoured books and poetry; George Patton played soldier; and Andrew Wyeth loved to draw and watch his father paint.

Connecting the Dots Backwards

Looking back, it seems obvious what each of these children

should grow up to accomplish. But it was not necessarily clear in the beginning. Beatrix Potter would never have dreamed she'd become a beloved author. Not one of Louis Armstrong's friends would have predicted his tremendous influence in jazz music and the entertainment industry.

Young people are always asked what they want to do when they grow up. If they know, that is fine; but if not, that's OK too. Putting pressure on a child or teen to set a goal and succeed at it before they have even discovered their passion serves anxious parents more than the youth. Sometimes the best thing a parent can do is just get out of the way. Children must be allowed to explore different interests and drop them when something new comes along. An early interest in building with Legos™ does not necessarily mean a child is destined to become an engineer. If they then become fascinated with horses, followed by monster movies, soccer, and puppetry—all is well.

Sometimes a succession of seemingly unrelated interests can come together in someone's ultimate career. Agatha Christie did a great deal of reading as a child, but she also loved amateur theatricals, cracking codes, riddle books, dressing in disguise with her big sister, playing the mandolin and piano, writing poetry and music, and finally writing detective stories at the age of eighteen. Her travels to Egypt and Paris as well as her work learning to be a pharmacist all found a way into her novels.

Your child may not know what he or she will do yet, but some time in the future it will all become clear. There's no telling what obscure fascination or experience will take hold of their imaginations.

In his famous 2005 Commencement Address at Stanford, Steve Jobs told his story about "connecting the dots." Jobs explained that he had no idea what he wanted to do with his life in college, so rather than waste his parents' money on tuition, he dropped out of Reed College and began sitting in on courses he was actually interested in.

At the time, Reed College had one of the best courses in calligraphy in the country, and the beautiful hand-lettered posters around campus attracted him so he took the course. Here he learned about different fonts and great typography even though it seemed to have no practical purpose. But ten years later when he was designing the Mac, he remembered those lessons and incorporated the multiple typefaces and font spacing into the display—a huge improvement over Windows. To the graduates he said:

> Of course it was impossible to connect the dots looking forward when I was in college, but it was very, very clear looking backwards ten years later. Again, you can't connect the dots looking forward. You can only connect them looking backwards, so you have to trust that the dots will somehow connect in your future. You have to trust in something—your gut, destiny, life, karma, whatever—because believing that the dots will connect down the road will give you the confidence to follow your heart, even when it leads you off the well-worn path, and that will make all the difference.[1]

Initiative vs. Discipline

How often have you heard parents lament over their child's lack of initiative? "She won't do anything unless I tell her a hundred times!" or, "If I let him he would just sit and watch TV all day." Notice, though, that what the parent really wants is for the child to do what the parent wants. This is really discipline and should not be confused with personal initiative. If you think about it, the ideals of parental discipline and youthful initiative are often at odds with one another. If a child is accustomed to doing and behaving just as Mother says, then any independent action becomes *de facto* rebellion.

> "You cannot build character and courage by taking away man's initiative and independence."
>
> —Abraham Lincoln

I once knew a family with two meek, obedient little girls. The mother lovingly controlled every minute of their day, ensuring they ate their salads, flossed after every meal, finished piles of homeschool work, and followed a daily schedule of rest, chores, exercise, and playtime. But this liberated mother's greatest woe was that her daughters would not speak up in a group—they showed no initiative, and they would not start anything on their own. To me, it seemed obvious that the girls had hardly any practice with personal initiative. Anytime a choice was presented to them, they looked to their mother to see which they should choose.

Part of it is temperament. Some children seem to have more of an independent streak than others and it would take a heap of discipline to make them behave as the two meek little girls did. But there is a fine line between discipline and micromanagement, just as there is a difference between loving and smothering. Everybody's situation is different.

My husband came up with a good analogy for our two very different boys. The oldest, who reminded us of Calvin from the *Calvin and Hobbes* comic strip, was like steel. He required the disciplinary equivalent of hammer and fire to make any impression on him. Our second son was sweet, obliging, and very sensitive. He was like clay. If he ever needed correction, the slightest suggestion was all it took, just a little gentle shaping.

Again, there is a fine line between appropriate discipline and micromanaging your kids. A certain amount of correction and guidance is necessary, but kids also need a good dose of freedom to practice initiative and decision-making. Since every family is different, you will have to decide where your line is.

Responsibility

It is amazing what kids are capable of doing when given real responsibility. The feminist reformer and publicist Gloria Steinem had a tough childhood caring for her mentally ill mother Ruth. In her younger years, the family traveled so much that Gloria rarely went to school; but after Ruth left her husband, they settled in Ohio and Gloria began going to school in sixth grade. The house they lived in was subdivided and they lived on the rent from two apartments. There were rats infesting the deteriorating house, and they never had enough money. Throughout this time, Gloria took care of her mother, got her schoolwork done, tap danced in nightclubs for $10 a night, and worked as a salesgirl when she was old enough.

Gloria knew that her mother loved her but could not take care of her. She later wrote: "For many years, I ... never imagined my mother any way other than ... someone to be worried about and cared for; an invalid who lay in bed with eyes closed and lips moving in occasional response to voices only she could hear."[2]

Gloria Steinem
1934 -
Feminist, journalist, civil rights activist, co-founder of Ms. magazine

Fortunately, Gloria maintained her amiable father's optimistic spirit and was determined to do better. She brought home comfort in the form of books from the library. She especially loved Louisa May Alcott. She also escaped her reality with frequent daydreams of saving someone at the last minute or saving the day.

When Gloria was entering her senior year of high school, her father offered to care for Ruth so that his daughter might finish school in Washington D.C. with her much older sister.

This was Gloria's big break—her freedom. She later went on to college and a life of activism.

Just as young Eli Whitney took over the care of his younger siblings when their mother became bedridden, Gloria Steinem knew there was no one else to care for her mother. She rose to the responsibility, however reluctantly. There are loads of kids who have been placed in these difficult situations and pulled through—though they have essentially been robbed of their carefree childhoods. I don't recommend this amount of responsibility to anyone, but it shows just how capable kids really are.

Making Choices—Wise or Unwise

Personal initiative is similar to work ethic but it extends to how we choose to use our time and solve problems. If we never have time of our own to choose how to spend, or problems of our own to choose how to solve, then we get very little practice with either. It would be far better for our kids to have practice and make their mistakes before they leave home.

If you agree in principle that kids ought to have a certain amount of autonomy, but fear that they will do nothing productive, try redefining your idea of "productive." No one who knew Walt Whitman as a child thought he would amount to much because he daydreamed all the time. Filmmaker Quentin Tarantino spent all of his free time watching movies. Writer Margaret Atwood loved to read comic books. Don't despair if your child doesn't write a sonata by the age of six or start his own business at the age of twelve. Some seeds take longer to germinate than others.

> *"In the long run, we shape our lives, and we shape ourselves. The process never ends until we die. And the choices we make are ultimately our own responsibility."*
>
> —Eleanor Roosevelt

Success gurus are correct in pointing out that successful

140

adults tend to have one unifying goal or vision that drives them. But kids are different. We adults are better off directing our energies to a carefully chosen goal than squandering them on every little emergency or distraction that comes our way. But kids have plenty of energy to squander. They can afford to skip around exploring different passions in their natural quest for learning. If they find what they're looking for—the vision that inspires them—great! But it may take some longer than others. They may need more experience or more opportunities to find what they want to do with their lives.

Remember This:

- Setting goals is very important for adults, but not necessarily for kids. They are still in the "figuring out who I am" phase.
- Sometimes it is difficult to connect the dots forward. Have faith that your teens will discover their passion when given the freedom to do so.
- Kids need a certain amount of latitude to practice initiative. They need practice making their own decisions and solving their own problems.
- A little responsibility trains a child for more responsibility, and so on. Kids are far more capable than we give them credit for.
- Find the right balance between parental and child control.
- Every family is different, so having conscious discussions between parents and children about responsibility and freedom is important. In order for kids to step up to the plate, Mom and Dad have to get out of the way.

Chapter Ten
Molting Time

"What molting time is to the birds, so adversity or misfortune is to us humans.

—Vincent van Gogh

What would you expect from a kid who grows up singing in brothels? Or a kid who skips school to make trouble and fight? Or a kid who spends months chipping away stone at the bottom of a 90-foot well? Kids like this become determined—determined never to do those things again.

Obviously there are a lot of kids who suffer from difficult childhoods and don't make anything positive from the experience. Adversity can lead to illness, depression, addiction, and destructive behavior—but it can also make us stronger. Combined with a positive mental attitude, at least one strong mentor, and a strong work ethic, adversity can spur determination like nothing else. Every child I studied suffered in some way: illness, loss, poverty, or neglect. Some had tragic childhoods.

Irving Berlin

Composer Irving Berlin grew up with his immigrant family in the squalid poverty of the Lower East Side in New York City. Although his father had been a respected Jewish cantor in Russia, he could not find equivalent work in the U.S. so he became a housepainter. His mother worked as a midwife and all his siblings worked in sweatshops, but still there was barely enough money to feed the family. After his father died and Irving turned fourteen, he left home to avoid burdening his mother.

Irving lived on the streets, singing for money in the saloons and brothels of Tin Pan Alley. His only goal was survival and to find some way out of there. He had learned to sing from his father, and learned what he could of piano from the other "buskers" in Chinatown. But it was his knack for writing witty, people-pleasing songs that got him noticed and eventually led to his great success.

Bernard Kerik

Bernard Kerik, who grew up to be the New York City Police Commissioner in 2000, had another rough childhood. His alcoholic mother left her husband and became a prostitute, leaving him with a series of acquaintances and relatives. When his father was finally able to get custody, he never saw his mother again.

His father and stepmother cared for him, but they were often exhausted from work. They lived in a rough New Jersey neighborhood where fighting and crime were common. Bernard hated feeling vulnerable and became obsessed with learning martial arts. He became known as a troublemaker, stealing money from his parents and skipping school to attend martial arts classes 25 miles away in New York City.

Once he got good at fighting, he had to fight less at school because he earned a reputation as someone to avoid. He earned a black belt in two and a half years because of his dedication:

> For the first time in my life I had ambition and drive and I was inspired. But it didn't all come from within. I had great teachers, and one of the greatest was Keith Keller, a tae kwon do instructor from Paterson, who was the first man to take a personal interest in me. It wasn't about money. It wasn't about business. He believed in me. And because he believed in me, I wanted desperately to live up to and to exceed his expectations . . . I was a young man who was given the gift of guidance, a young man in dire need of direction and discipline. And he gave it to me.[1]

Bernard hated school, and at the age of fifteen he tricked his stepmother into signing a slip allowing him to dropout. He then went to work at a moving company and later at his father's machine shop. But he didn't like the grind of work either. All he wanted to do was fight, so at age eighteen he joined the army, hoping to get to Korea and study tae kwon do.

Boot camp was difficult but he handled it well. Bernard was already in great shape and he claimed that the "mental side—the discipline and the challenge—was something I had been craving without even realizing it. My father's concern that I was too soft or lazy or undisciplined turned out to be completely wrong. The military was the first time that life made sense to me—here was a code, a sense of honor and duty."[2]

> *"One who gains strength by overcoming obstacles possesses the only strength which can overcome adversity."*
>
> —Albert Schweitzer

John Muir

Naturalist John Muir acknowledged the benefits of his rough childhood in the schoolyards of Scotland. At the time, school and church lessons were enforced by whipping, and every boy was expected to fight every other boy in town to determine pecking order. Muir wrote:

> All these various thrashings, however, were admirably influential in developing not only our memory but fortitude as well. For if we did not endure our school punishments and fighting pains without flinching and making faces, we were mocked on the playground, and public opinion on a Scotch playground was a powerful agent in controlling behavior; therefore we at length managed to keep our features in smooth repose while enduring pain that would try anybody but an American Indian.[3]

Enduring pain was a useful skill for would-be soldiers (as all of Muir's school chums wished to be), but it also gave Muir the strength to endure the next ten years of his life. When he was eleven, his family immigrated to Wisconsin and began the backbreaking work of building a homestead. As the oldest boy, his strict Calvinist father worked him relentlessly. Every moment of the day he was chopping, plowing, planting, mowing, and following his father's orders. For months he worked every day by himself chipping away stone to dig a 90-foot well. His father would not let him out until dark—he almost died from "choke-damp." The hard work and lack of sleep and food ultimately stunted his growth.

The only time John had for himself was in the middle of the night. He trained himself to wake at one in the morning so that he could study and build things in his cellar workshop until dawn. He invented a self-setting sawmill, water wheels, door locks and latches, thermometers, hygrometers, pyrometers, clocks, a barometer, a horse feeder, and an alarm clock.

Muir's greatest love, though, was the outdoors and he seized every opportunity to hunt, fish, or pick berries with his mother. The wildness of the fields and forests was a balm to his soul—his ultimate comfort.

At the age of 21, John Muir was legally emancipated and left his father's house, never to return. He worked and paid his way through four years of university, then after graduation, used his engineering skills employed in a machine shop. All seemed to be well until an accidental injury to his eye left him blinded for months. He thought he may never see properly again, and realized his greatest regret would be missing the wonders of nature. When his eye healed, he quit his machine shop job and left in search of "wildness."

> John Muir
> 1838 - 1914
> *Naturalist, explorer, author, conservationist, instrumental in creation of Yosemite National Park, co-founder of Sierra Club*

Without all of his suffering, John Muir may very well have stayed on the family farm or at the machine shop. He may never have traveled to the mountains of California and founded the Sierra Club, or wrote his luminous books, or helped preserve Yosemite Valley as a national park.

One hopes that no one should have to suffer the way Irving Berlin, Bernard Kerik, or John Muir did, but it is true that their ordeals provoked a singularity of purpose: determination to survive, escape, and pursue their dreams.

If life had been easy for those boys, would they have found the same success? We can only speculate, but when success guru Orison Swett Marden interviewed John D. Rockefeller, the farmboy-turned-oil tycoon, Rockefeller praised adversity:

> 'To my mind,' he said, 'There is something unfortunate in being born in a city. Most young men raised in New York and other large centers have not had the struggles which come to us who were reared in the country. It is a noticeable fact that the country men

are crowding out the city fellows who have wealthy fathers. They are willing to do more work and go through more for the sake of winning success in the end. Sons of wealthy parents haven't a ghost of a show in competition with the fellow who come from the country with a determination to do something in the world.'[4]

Who Gets Weak? Who Gets Stronger?

Not all of the famous homeschoolers I studied had such difficult beginnings, but they all had some obstacle, deprivation, or pain to overcome. Poverty, hunger, illness, and loss of loved ones were common. Friedrich Nietzsche's famous quote, "That which does not kill us makes us stronger," seems to be true for those I studied; but we all know of people who instead succumb to adversity through addiction or destructive behaviors. Why the difference?

There are many ways to face down hardship, but the difference between growth and giving up lies again in a *positive mental attitude*—the foundation of everything. As discussed in Chapter Seven, a positive mental attitude is something that can be developed, but it is difficult without help. Unconditional love and support from someone, plus mentoring, makes all the difference. Kids need to see what a positive attitude looks like, if not from a family member then from a coach, teacher, or some other youth leader. They also need to see the possibility of success—or at least escape.

Irving Berlin had hard-working loving parents, plus the older "buskers" to teach him the business. Bernard Kerik had martial arts and military instructors who believed in him and gave him the discipline he needed to thrive. John Muir had a devoted mother and a self-acquired education to show him how to escape his father.

Another part of surviving adversity is having something to love, which gives us something to live for. Berlin loved to sing, Kerik loved martial arts, and Muir loved the wilderness. They all had something worthy to hang on to even in the worst of conditions. For many of the children I studied, books provided the escape and hope for the future. For some, it was art, music, sports, or faith.

Learning From Adversity

As much as we may want to protect our kids from suffering, it is important to remember that a little hardship can be a good thing. Just as gardeners place a gently blowing fan near indoor seedlings, then gradually "harden them off" with increasing intervals of time outdoors, we need to gradually give our kids more opportunities to get stronger.

I'm not suggesting that we make our children miserable just to toughen them up. We should just make them less comfortable. Don't always do things for them that they could do for themselves. Confidence grows with self-reliance. Infants, of course, are wholly dependent on their parents and they should be given all the love, help, and support they need. But as they get older, nature has provided children with the proper instinct to play, learn, and "do it myself." They need to use their hands: touching, folding, drawing, cutting, opening, closing, pushing buttons, stirring, kneading, holding, pouring. If they are having trouble, don't "rescue" them unless they ask. Even then, don't necessarily take over the job. Maybe all they need is feedback or encouragement.

> *"I can assure you that there is the greatest practical benefit in making a few failures early in life."*
> —Thomas H. Huxley

I learned a lesson about underestimating what kids can do

when my second son was four years old. I was busy getting ready for an office party at our house and had been cleaning all day. By the time I started getting the food ready in the afternoon I knew I was behind schedule and starting to get a little frantic. When my sweet little boy asked if he could help me, my first instinct was to refuse because I was too busy to show him what he could do. For-

> *"Adversity is the midwife of genius."*
> —Napoleon Bonaparte

tunately, I stopped myself and asked him to help me assemble the tray we were going to use for a sandwich buffet. I set him up on a stool at the counter in front of a large platter and gave him about four pounds of assorted lunchmeat and cheeses. I showed him how to roll up the slices and arrange them in nice overlapping layers, then left him to it while I worked on something else. About twenty minutes later, he proudly announced, "All done! Look, Mommy!" I was flabbergasted—he had done a beautiful job! I had fully expected to finish the job myself when he lost interest, but here he had done the whole thing himself. He beamed with pleasure, satisfied with his own work and happy to have helped me.

There are plenty of opportunities throughout childhood to safely allow kids to fend for themselves (and others). In the beginning it may be getting dressed on their own or slicing their own bananas over cereal. Later it might mean caring for animals, picking up groceries, or doing their own laundry. If they want to build a doghouse, show them how to use the saw and drill and stand back. Teens especially need challenges. Teach them how to use public transportation. Have them fill out their own paperwork for camps, classes, jobs, etc. Task them with calling local auto parts stores to compare prices on brake pads, for instance.

Besides learning basic life skills, kids should have the opportunity to get really good at something they are interested in: horseback riding, music, dancing, programming, sports, art, robots, debating, drama, martial arts, 4H, backpacking, rock climbing, etc. It's OK if kids want to try different things and drop one activity for another activity, but ultimately they should settle on one pursuit and go for it. The dedication to practice and training will serve them well in all of their future endeavors because they'll remember what it feels like. They'll remember that they are capable of such an effort.

Organized activities requiring training are effective because they cannot be faked. Competition and coaches demand effort. If the student practices hard, they will get better. The resulting self-esteem is real—not engineered.

Unfortunately, there are a lot of youth programs, designed by well-meaning adults, which seem to be entirely based on a tier of artificial awards, incentives, and catchy slogans. The focus is all about jumping through the next hoop to get the next award, rather than any meaningful improvement. These are OK for social gatherings, but don't let these fake endeavors take the place of real endeavors. The goal is mastery—not a certificate of recognition.

Like molting, adversity is necessary for growth. It brings out the strength, determination, and special skills in one's character. Some suffering, such as illness, loss, poverty, and family trauma may be outside our control, but how we respond to it is up to us. Maintaining a positive attitude and providing unconditional love and support to our children can make all the difference.

> *"I don't measure a man's success by how high he climbs but how high he bounces when he hits bottom."*
>
> —General George Patton

Remember This:

- Muscles don't get stronger unless they're worked. Adversity is the ultimate personal trainer.
- Youth are best able to overcome adversity with a positive mental attitude, mentoring, and something (or someone) to love.
- Allow your kids the blessings of discomfort. Let them work; let them make mistakes; let them be bored; let them earn their own money—all in the spirit of love and good humor, of course.
- Opportunities for distinction (grades, awards, praise) are not nearly the same thing as opportunities for mastery.
- Protecting, coddling, and micromanaging young people undermines their ability to accomplish anything truly difficult. Give them a chance!

Part Three

Atmosphere

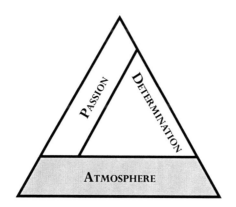

Chapter Eleven
Keep it Real

"A house is not a home unless it contains food and fire for the mind as well as the body."

—Benjamin Franklin

So far we have looked at what parents should or should not do to help rouse passion and determination. But underlying both is the growing child's atmosphere of home and community. Atmosphere is like the dirt a plant digs its roots into, full of rich nutrients and support. You might think that I am about to recommend a carefully prepared child-centered home complete with enriching toys and learning materials, but that's not the idea. Children learn about their world by living in it, and by copying the people around them. The best atmosphere for a child is an authentic one—one that reflects the actual interests and occupations of the family. Kids need to spend time with adults as well as other children, having conversations, going places, and doing interesting things.

It's particularly important that the parents continue exploring, creating, and learning for their own purposes. The overwhelming majority of famous homeschoolers I studied grew up in homes where learning was encouraged and modeled. Teddy Roosevelt is one example.

Teddy Roosevelt

Teddy was born in 1859 and was taught at home with his three siblings by his aunt. The Roosevelts were a tight-knit clan who all lived near each other, and Teddy's only outside playmates were cousins or children of old family friends. Teddy's father, nicknamed "Greatheart" by the family, was authoritative but affectionate. Every morning he would say prayers with the children on the sofa. He taught them to ride horses and climb trees. He invited interesting new people such as John Hay and Matthew Arnold over for dinner and encouraged the children to listen to the conversations.

Teddy thrived in the company of his large extended family, particularly visits from his Uncle Hilborne, who took the time to talk with inquisitive Teddy about subjects dear to his heart—science and natural history. His sister Conie remembered their uncle:

> The very fact that he was not achieving a thousand worthwhile things, as was my father, the very fact that he was not busied with the practical care and thought for us, as were my mother and aunt, brought about between us that delightful relationship when the older person leads rather than drives the younger into paths of literature and learning.[1]

The children loved the outdoors, and Teddy filled his notebooks with drawings and descriptions of ants, birds, spiders, beetles, mice, and dragonflies. On a year-long family trip to Europe in 1869 and a trip down the Nile in 1872, he filled more notebooks with detailed notes about the museums and natural wonders they visited.

Writing to his mother from Harvard, Roosevelt wrote: "It seems perfectly wonderful, in looking back over my eighteen years of existence, to see how I have literally never spent an unhappy day, unless by my own fault!"[2]

Trips to Europe and the Nile are fine for those who can afford them, but the key elements of Roosevelt's home atmosphere were his strong supportive family members, opportunities for good conversation, books to read, and places to explore.

"Education is an Atmosphere, a Discipline, a Life"

Charlotte Mason recognized the value of atmosphere in education. The motto of the Parents' Union she created was "Education is an atmosphere, a discipline, a life." She explains in her books that a true education depends on all three of these factors. Her idea of a proper atmosphere is *not* one specially made for children. Children should live amongst the same people and things of their family—not sheltered in a hothouse environment as if they were fragile orchids. Mason describes atmosphere as a breath of fresh living air, exposed to the tumbles of ordinary life. A child that is too pampered and fussed over is made weak.

"Education is a discipline" as described by Miss Mason is the cultivation of good habits, which I will get to in the next chapter. The third component of her motto, "Education is a life," refers to the need for real, vital ideas to feed a person's mind. Just as wholesome nourishing food is required for the body to live, whole nourishing ideas are required for the mind. Here is where Mason's famous penchant for "living books" comes in. She claims that typical schoolbooks and moralizing storybooks are nothing but "twaddle," devoid of any real meaty concepts to chew on. Real education comes from original thought. Part of an atmosphere of learning is access to good books. Even if we don't buy the books, we can at least make regular trips to the library and let the child choose what to read. Mason advises us that the child ". . . is an eclectic; he may choose this or that; our business is to supply him with due abundance and variety and his to take what he needs."[3]

The Wright Brothers' parents kept an eclectic library of authors such as Irving, Hawthorne, Scott, Grimm, Andersen, and Gibbon. It also included multivolume histories of England and France, natural history books, *The Spectator*, two sets of encyclopedias, and Plutarch's *Lives*—a favorite of Wilbur's. Mr. Wright also kept a large collection of theology books for use in preparing his sermons. All of it was available to the children.

Charlotte Mason didn't think kids should hole up inside all day reading books, though. She also believed that children should spend a great deal of time outside in nature and visiting places. They need to form personal connections with people, animals, things, art, skills, and thoughts found in their natural environment.

The famous homeschoolers I studied certainly fit this pattern. Beatrix Potter spent winter months visiting the natural history and art museums, and the summer months exploring the Scottish countryside. Pearl Buck spent hours visiting with her Chinese neighbors. Robert Frost worked as a messenger boy in the rough frontier town of San Francisco. Samuel Clemens (Mark Twain) enjoyed an exuberant boyhood on the banks of the Mississippi River. Louis Armstrong practically lived on the streets of his New Orleans neighborhood. Irving Berlin roamed and worked the streets of Manhattan's Lower East Side.

> *"Basically, I believe the world is a jungle, and if it's not a bit of a jungle in the home, a child cannot possibly be fit to enter the outside world."*
>
> —Bette Davis

158

These were not sheltered or coddled children. They experienced life—even some of the ugly parts. These experiences certainly found their way into the work each of these people did. Beatrix Potter's explorations became *Peter Rabbit*; Pearl Buck and Samuel Clemens picked up the dialects and characters for their future books; Robert Frost's observations appeared in his poetry; Louis Armstrong and Irving Berlin transformed the energy of the streets into their music.

"Education is a life," means that learning doesn't stop just because we turn 18 or 21 or "graduate." Kids should witness their grandparents, parents, community mentors, or anyone else they know doing and learning new things. That's what puts the zest in living. Mrs. Wright, mother of Orville and Wilbur, was very handy with tools and liked to build things. Pierre Curie's father included his children in his work at the Museum of Natural History and his humanitarian efforts to help wounded soldiers. Mary Leakey's father was fascinated with Egyptology and archeology.

Another example comes from anthropologist Margaret Mead. Her whole family valued education, but her college-educated grandmother was particularly sensitive to the value of home life and thought that every child should grow up on a farm. Mead later wrote:

> So the overriding academic ethos shaped all our lives. This was tempered by my mother's sense of responsibility for society, by my father's greater interest in real processes than in theoretical abstractions, and by my grandmother's interest in real children, in chickens, and in how to season stewed tomatoes with toasted bread.[4]

"Natural" environment means one that is not contrived. It is one that the family has arranged to meet the needs and comfort of all members, not just the children. Nicholas Humphrey, a theoretical psychologist, wrote about his childhood:

> As children, we lived and breathed science, though of course we didn't know this at the time. Our sprawling basement rooms were full of apparatus: prototype engines of my grandfather's, pumps and torpedoes, lathes and jigsaws, Meccano sets, photographic apparatus, Wimshurst electrical machines, microscopes, aquariums."[5]

Humphrey grew up in a large extended family of scientists who *did* things with the children. The children could participate or not as they saw fit. "What I gained from this childhood environment was a sense of intellectual entitlement—a right to ask questions, to pry, to provoke, to go where I pleased in pursuit of knowledge."[6]

Another scientist, Alison Gopnik, wrote: "For me, intellectual life wasn't something you achieved, it was something you breathed. I never felt 'enriched,' though I did sometimes notice that other kids seemed oddly, peculiarly impoverished, and I was happy."[7]

> *"The best compliment to a child or a friend is the feeling you give him that he has been set free to make his own inquiries, to come to conclusions that are right for him, whether or not they coincide with your own."*
>
> —Alistair Cooke

These families did not artificially "enrich" their environment for purposes of child development, but naturally created an environment based on their own interests, aesthetics, and intellectual needs.

Our home is crammed with the books and paraphernalia of our family's various interests: woodworking, gardening, building canoes, dog-sledding, rock-climbing, motorcycles, kite-surfing, cooking, paddling, drawing, hiking, photography, guitar, computer programming, yoga, martial arts, skate-boarding, history, herbalism, Shakespeare, sewing, and reading and learning of all kinds. It's a ridiculous hodgepodge of stuff and makes us laugh to see it all. But it's authentic; each layer represents a passing or lasting fascination of some kind. Best of all is the collection of friends we have met pursuing these interests. Because of this, our kids have met great people from around the world and a variety of backgrounds.

Conversation

Besides continual learning, great books and time outdoors, another feature of a successful home atmosphere is conversation. The Roosevelt children enjoyed time with adults, both listening to and participating in conversations. Young Beatrix Potter was too shy to participate, but she hid under the drawing room table to listen to her spirited grandmother conversing with guests. Archeologist Mary Leakey and her well-educated father had long after-dinner conversations, and she was introduced to many interesting people during their world travels. Her taste for real conversation about such weighty subjects as Egyptology, art, and archeology spoiled her when her father died and her mother attempted to send her to school. She found the atmosphere of school insipid and tedious and was expelled so often that her mother finally gave up and let her acquire her own education attending lectures.

The authors of *Cradles of Eminence* found in their research of 700 famous men and women that:

> Whatever the family climate of opinion, being treated as an adult is incomparably important to a young child who is intellectually capable. When he receives an audience and can speak and be spoken to, he is emotionally, as well as intellectually, satisfied by the experience.[8]

Homeschoolers have an advantage over kids at school because they naturally will have more time and attention from the adults in their lives. They spend the better part of the day with the homeschooling parent, and in the typically busy after-school hours, their homework is already done so they have time for extracurricular activities and hanging out with the rest of the family.

Besides promoting emotional well-being, intelligent conversation promotes learning. When children are able to discuss the books they are reading, ask questions, or share their theories about current events, it helps them to process and remember their thoughts. They also learn the subtle rules of etiquette for effective speaking and listening. Adults are usually polite and have learned not to interrupt or dominate a conversation, or to attack a person when they disagree. Children pick up on this when given a chance. It also helps them to think about other sides of an issue, as friends and family invariably have different opinions. Inviting interesting guests over for dinner is a great way for kids to learn about new things and hear new perspectives. Cooperative study groups or book clubs can also encourage stimulating conversation.

Public school advocates often say that homeschooled children are too sheltered and that they need to go to school to be exposed to different opinions and be properly "socialized." I think the real fear is that kids will turn out too much like their parents, and not the way the state officials would prefer to mold citizens. But really, expecting kids to learn social skills primarily from other kids their own age is like asking a roomful of beginning dancers to learn ballet from one another. Yes, they should have opportunities to play and socialize without parents hovering over them,

> *"The greatest compliment that was ever paid me was when one asked me what I thought, and attended to my answer."*
>
> —Henry David Thoreau

but it needs to be balanced by ample opportunities to speak with adults.

If a child truly feels stifled and bored at home, then perhaps public or private school will fill the void. But in many ways, the school environment isn't real. It is an environment constructed by officials for the sole purpose of indoctrinating, minding, and molding students. It can be en-

> *"I just owe almost everything to my father and it's passionately interesting for me that the things that I learned in a small town, in a very modest home, are just the things that I believe have won the election."*
>
> —Margaret Thatcher

tertaining, with plenty of drama and social intrigue. It can provide valuable access to books and instruction that many children would not otherwise receive. But it is not an environment that otherwise exists in real life. Here the occupants are placed in groups, working for artificial rewards to learn something that someone else has deemed important, following a daily routine designed more for crowd control and administrative efficiency than personal fulfillment.

Life is wonderful. Real life, real work, real people with real interests, problems, and stories—that's what inspires passion and determination. That's what sticks in our memories. Stewed tomatoes and torpedoes in the basement beat cafeteria culture any day.

Remember This:

- Atmosphere provides the raw material for life and creativity, and is a vital part of home education.
- Students thrive in homes where adults value learning, read books, and pursue their own passions but who also take the time to do things with their kids. They take their kids to interesting places and introduce them to new people.

• A healthy learning environment does not revolve around the children, but includes them in it.

• If parents are able to afford it, it's great to support a child's interests with quality tools such as a telescope, easel, or a workbench, but there is no need to obsess over "enrichment."

• Great books (from the library) and stimulating conversation are free—and the best investment you will ever make.

• Real life trumps artificial enrichment and "socialization."

Chapter Twelve
Habit Power

"Excellence is an art won by training and habituation. We do not act rightly because we have virtue or excellence, but we rather have those because we have acted rightly. We are what we repeatedly do. Excellence, then, is not an act but a habit."

—Aristotle

Ben Franklin was a guy who understood the power of habits. He started out life with no great advantages. His father was a humble chandler with seventeen other children to care for, but Ben was determined to better himself. He worked hard, read books, practiced writing, conducted experiments, and got in plenty of trouble. But most of all, he paid attention. He understood human nature and his own personal failings. So he created his own self-improvement plan. As a young man, he developed his now famous list of thirteen virtues to follow (see sidebar on next page).

Franklin attempted to integrate these virtues by keeping a small notebook with a weekly grid to mark his transgressions. He tried to focus particular effort on one virtue a week so that by the end of thirteen weeks he would have mastered each virtue.

Ben Franklin's List of Virtues:

Temperance: *Eat not to dullness. Drink not to elevation.*

Silence: *Speak not but what may benefit others or yourself. Avoid trifling conversation.*

Order: *Let all your things have their places. Let each part of your business have its time.*

Resolution: *Resolve to perform what you ought. Perform without fail what you resolve.*

Frugality: *Make no expense but to do good to others or yourself: i.e., Waste nothing.*

Industry: *Lose no time. Be always employed in something useful. Cut off all unnecessary actions.*

Sincerity: *Use no hurtful deceit. Think innocently and justly; and if you speak, speak accordingly.*

Justice: *Wrong none, by doing injuries or omitting the benefits that are your duty.*

Moderation: *Avoid extremes. Forbear resenting injuries so much as you think they deserve.*

Cleanliness: *Tolerate no uncleanness in body, clothes or habitation.*

Tranquility: *Be not disturbed at trifles, or at accidents common or unavoidable.*

Chastity: *Rarely use venery but for health or offspring; never to dullness, weakness or the injury of your own or another's peace or reputation.*

Humility: *Imitate Jesus and Socrates.*[1]

Needless to say, Franklin was not always successful and struggled with virtues such as temperance, chastity, and humility all his life. But he was conscious of it, and did his best.

It's admirable that Ben Franklin was aware of his faults and willing to change them, but changing habits from bad to good is very difficult. Notice how many of his listed virtues could easily get a better foothold in childhood: Temperance, order, frugality, sincerity, justice, moderation, and cleanliness. Really, all habits—good or bad—get their start in childhood. We owe it to our kids to pay attention to these things. It's odd that we homeschoolers should focus so much on academic achievement when children are already so naturally motivated to learn new things, but this then leaves us too exhausted to focus on the far-more-important *habits* of success. Which do you think will be more important in the long run?

I'm telling you right now that habits are a better predictor of success than any test score. The successful people I studied *worked* at it. They had character. Achievement didn't just fall in their laps because they were smart. They had disciplined themselves to work hard, follow through with promises, take responsibility, and manage their own personal behavior—not always perfectly, but consciously.

Remember Charlotte Mason's motto, "Education is an atmosphere, a discipline, a life"? The discipline part refers to good habits. Just as the at-

> *"Genius without character is mere friskiness."*
>
> —attributed to Ralph Waldo Emerson

mosphere of home and community intellectually influences children, the habits they learn there will influence their later productivity and effectiveness.

"Education is a discipline" does not mean hours of study chained to a desk. Miss Mason was not in favor of the typical schoolroom tactics of discipline, drill, and memorization. On the contrary, she believed that the right sort of lessons should be a delight, not a chore. The discipline she speaks of is in the formation of habits. Foremost is the habit of attention, followed by other habits of the mind, morals, religion, and physical development.

Mason believed that children were born good, but lacked the willpower to do the difficult or distasteful things. It was up to parents to cultivate these habits—not an easy thing, but one that must be attended to on a regular basis. Mason wrote: "The mother who takes pains to endow her children with good habits secures for herself smooth and easy days; while she who lets their habits take care of themselves has a weary life of endless friction with the children."[2]

The problem is, we all tend to choose behavior that is the easiest or provides the most instant gratification, until we grow wise enough to determine what behaviors are ultimately harmful. Unfortunately, we may not know how important the daily chore of brushing our teeth is until we have acquired a mouthful of cavities. After a painful visit to the dentist, we may then vow to brush regularly, but it would be much healthier to learn this habit before the damage is done. It's also better to learn the good habit before the bad habit sets in.

> *The second half of a man's life is made up of nothing but the habits he has acquired during the first half.*
>
> —Feodor Dostoevski

This applies to thoughts as well as behavior. In her book, *Formation of Character*, Charlotte Mason tells the story of a beloved teenage girl named Dorothy who was prone to sullen, morose fits of despair when things did not go her way. The consulting doctor explained to the worried parents:

> Now, these thoughts become automatic; they come of themselves, and spread and flow as a river makes and enlarges its bed. Such habit of thought is set up, and must go on indefinitely, in spite of struggles, un-less—and here is the word of hope—a contrary habit is set up, diverting the thoughts into some quite new channel. Keep the thoughts running briskly in the new channel, and, behold, the old connections are broken, whilst a new growth of brain substance is perpetually taking place.[3]

Dorothy had always showed this tendency for sulking, even as a child. The doctor told the parents that they should have taken the matter in hand long before it became a habit. He explained that the only way to overcome the negative thought pattern was to catch it early and replace it with a new positive thought. Dorothy was very unhappy with herself and perfectly willing to try whatever the doctor suggested, though she claimed it was impossible to change her thoughts when she was possessed by that dark mood.

The doctor told her:

This is how it works. When ill thoughts *begin* to molest you, turn away your mind with a vigorous turn, and *think of something else.* I don't mean think good, forgiving thoughts, perhaps you are not ready for that yet; but think of something interesting and pleasant; the new dress you must plan, the friend you like best, the book you are reading; best of all, fill heart and mind suddenly with some capital plan for giving pleasure to some poor body whose days are dull. The more exciting the thing you think of, the safer you are. Never mind about fighting the evil thought. This is the one thing you have to do; for this is, perhaps, the sole power the will has. [italics in the original][4]

The trick is to avert the unwanted behavior quickly and keep at it consistently for two to three months, until the new behavior takes hold.

The Habit of Attention

Mason relates another story of frustrated parents writing her a letter asking for advice regarding their daughter Kitty. The endearing six year old was very bright, but she drove her family crazy with dawdling and her tendency to flit from one thing to the next without finishing what she started, even in play.

Mason wrote back to them, first acknowledging the problem at hand. "But it is true; these naughty, winsome ways of Kitty's will end in her growing up like half the 'girls'—that is, young women—one meets. They talk glibly on many subjects; but test them, and they know nothing of any; they are ready to undertake anything, but they carry nothing through."[5]

Mason then explains:

First, as to her lessons: you *must* help her to gain the power of attention; that should have been done long

169

ago, but better late than never, and an aunt who has given her mind to these matters takes blame to herself for not having seen the want sooner. 'But,' I fancy you are saying, 'if the child has no faculty of attention, how can we give it to her? It's just a natural defect.' Not a bit of it! Attention is not a faculty at all, though I believe it is worth more than all the so-called faculties put together; this, at any rate, is true, that no talent, no genius, is worth much without the power of attention; and this is the power which makes men or women successful in life.[6]

Mason's remedy was to get Kitty in the habit of attention by keeping her lessons very short (no more than ten minutes) and interesting. Instead of working a page of sums, she could add and subtract dominoes, but at the end of ten minutes it is done. "Then, vary the lessons; now head, and now hands; now tripping feet and tuneful tongue; but in every lesson let Kitty . . . carry away the joyous sense of—'Something attempted, something done.'"[7]

In this way, the distractible child develops the habit of attention in short, manageable bursts. I think this is a valid technique, especially with children who have legitimate attention problems, but it may harm the child who already knows how to focus. Just like young Pierre Curie hated to be interrupted when he was working on something, many children would not appreciate being told to stop what they are doing after ten minutes.

Maria Montessori recognized this. In her classrooms, the students were free to select the work they would do and continue for as long as they wished. But when they were done, they were expected to put the work away before moving on to something else. She believed that children would naturally pay attention to what they were interested in. The habit that Montessori teachers reinforce is children taking responsibility for what they do by selecting, then putting away, their chosen activity.

Modern children (and adults) may have an especially hard time developing the habit of attention because there are so many more distractions now. Video games, television, Facebook, texting, tweets, advertisements, radio, music players, and other electronic media all conspire against us in a frenetic pace of 30-second sound-bites. All of it competes for our attention. Ultimately, we all have to learn to decide what is worthy of our attention and what to tune out—or turn off. Young children are really helpless in this regard. It is very hard for them to ignore the colorful glitzy temptations that companies have so carefully created to entice us. As parents, we can't always filter what our kids see or hear out in the world, but we can be thoughtful about the quantity and quality of media that enters the home. I'll cover this subject more in depth in Chapter Fourteen.

Replacing Bad Habits

Different children may require different approaches to their bad habits, but the story of "Inconstant Kitty" helps us see what must be done. The only way to get rid of a bad habit is to replace it with a good one, little by little. Just like we get used to a new food by tasting it over a period of time, we can get used to a new habit. Children who are new to a Montessori classroom may not be in the habit of putting away their work, but after watching the other students and seeing consistent expectations from the teachers, it soon becomes a habit.

Creating a new habit is actually a lot of work. That's why so many people fail to do it. Like water, we all tend to follow the same easy, well-worn paths rather than exert the effort to clear a new path. But this is all the more reason to help our kids build the right paths in the first place. It takes diligence. And, of course, many of the habits our kids learn are learned by watching us. If we make a point of always arriving on time, saying "Thank you," admitting when we have made a mistake, exercising regularly, or cleaning up our messes, then those things will appear normal to a child.

We can reinforce those expectations with gentle reminders. But we will have to be consistent and follow through. It's not enough to just say, "Please put away your paints so we can set the table," then repeat it at regular intervals hoping that your child will comply. You will save yourself a lot of heartache if you get your child in the habit early of cleaning up her paints as soon as she is done. Do it with her every time at first. Show her how to clean the brushes and where to put her picture to dry and where to put the paint box every time. The hard part is consistency. Even if you are in the middle of preparing dinner or a phone call, you need to initiate the cleaning-up process as soon as she is done painting. Eventually your consistency will pay off and it will become a habit she can continue on her own.

Training

Building good habits works on the same principle as good training. In his book, *The Talent Code*, author Daniel Coyle presented the fascinating brain research being done on super-talented individuals. Neurologists have found that the more a nerve fires, the more myelin wraps around the nerve. And the more myelin that is built up along certain nerve pathways, the quicker the nerve impulses can travel. "Myelin is infrastructure all right, but with a powerful twist: within the vast metropolis of the brain, myelin quietly transforms narrow alleys into broad, lighting-fast super-highways. Neural traffic that once trundled along at two miles an hour can, with myelin's help, accelerate to two hundred miles an hour."[8]

But myelin super-highways aren't built overnight. They are built over time and with consistent targeted practice. Every time a guitarist strums a chord or a gym-nast pounces on a springboard, they are reinforcing certain neural path-ways. The pathways can either be cor-rect or incorrect, depending on the quality of the practice. That is why good teachers and coaches are always so particular about building skills in a certain order, and correcting form and posture before the student has a chance to practice (and thus reinforce) bad habits.

> *"If people knew how hard I had to work to gain my mastery, it would not seem so wonderful at all."*
>
> —Michelangelo

As an example, Coyle tells the story of two educational psy-chologists who were allowed to observe a famously effective basketball coach named John Wooden. Wooden had such an impressive long-term record of winning that ESPN later named him the greatest coach of all time in any sport. The research-ers were surprised to find that Wooden didn't act like any other coach they had ever seen. He didn't give long speeches, lessons, punishment, or praise. What he did do was run very short, in-tense drills accompanied by constant feedback and correction. His advice to each player would be very brief, such as "Do some dribbling between shots," or "Hard, driving, quick steps." The researchers recorded everything in their notebooks and later tal-lied it up: they "coded 2,326 discrete acts of teaching. Of them, a mere 6.9 percent were compliments. Only 6.6 percent were ex-pressions of displeasure. But 75 percent were pure information: what to do, how to do it, when to intensify an activity."[9]

Wooden also carefully planned each practice session with the intent of non-stop, intense, focused conditioning. He routinely demonstrated skills first the right way, then the wrong way, then again the right way. He even showed new players how to put on socks properly to avoid blisters. When the players practiced, he saw and corrected errors instantly.

Coyle wrote:

> Wooden may not have known about myelin, but like all master coaches, he had a deep understanding of how it worked. He taught in chunks, using what he called the 'whole-part method'—he would teach players an entire move, then break it down to work on its elemental actions. He formulated laws of learning (which might be retitled laws of myelin): explanation, demonstration, imitation, correction, and repetition. 'Don't look for the big, quick improvement. Seek the small improvement one day at a time. That's the only way it happens—and when it happens, it lasts,' he wrote in *The Wisdom of Wooden*."[10]

The Talent Code is a terrific book for anyone interested in the cultivation of talent—particularly musical or athletic. But for my purposes, it helps explain the cultivation of habits. Training for anything involves repetition of the correct behavior. Drama, screaming, and scolding are not helpful. Consistency, modeling, and patience are the way to go. It also helps to break the new skill or habit into "chunks," perfecting one bit at a time until the whole is learned.

When Benjamin Franklin created his self-improvement plan, he attempted to master his list of thirteen virtues by focusing on one virtue per week. This was probably too ambitious a schedule, which may explain why he didn't master all of them. New habits take a while to form. But Franklin made a solid effort, which surely helped his later success. People trusted his opinions because he had a reputation for honesty, hard work, and an even temper.

Which Habits?

In her books, Charlotte Mason valued Victorian habits such as diligence, reverence, gentleness, truthfulness, promptness, neatness, and courtesy. Success guru Orison Swett Marden valued persistence most, followed by: physical and mental vigor achieved through proper rest, recreation, diet, and exercise; decisiveness; the urge to better one's best; honesty ("The Backbone of Manhood"); getting work done no matter how disagreeable; spending time on self-improvement and constant learning.

The famous homeschoolers I studied matched Marden's list better than Mason's list of habits. They were not necessarily models of Victorian propriety. In fact Charlotte Mason would have been shocked by some of them—such as Benjamin Franklin (if she had known his whole story). Qualities such as reverence, gentleness, promptness, and neatness were practiced by some of my subjects (Pearl Buck, Horace Greeley, and John Burroughs for instance), but not all. Most inventors were not known for their neatness. The artists, musicians, and poets were not known for their reverence (by Christian standards anyway). The main difference seems to be sheer feistiness. Thomas Edison, Irving Berlin, Frederick Douglass, Mary Leakey, and the others got ahead because they were bold, and a little stubborn. They broke free of convention. But all of them were masters of determination and self-education.

Mason's list of virtues is still undoubtedly important for emotional, moral, and social success. Neatness and courtesy extend to all the little things we do to live amicably together, such as not interrupting, sharing the last slice of pizza, keeping promises, closing doors quietly, and throwing the empty milk carton away instead of putting it back in the refrigerator. These are all worthy things to teach our children—but be careful not to civilize the spunk right out of them.

It All Starts With You

No pressure or anything—but just as kids learn a positive attitude, work ethic, and self-discipline by watching you, they will also pick up on your habits, and the habits of other adults and children around them (or on TV). They will notice everything, good or bad, so *someone* has to model and reinforce proper habits if we want our children to learn them.

It could be a teacher or coach. C.S. Lewis was profoundly influenced by a favorite teacher at Wyvern College, who treated every student with the utmost courtesy and respect, and expected the same behavior amongst his students. "Thus, even had he taught us nothing else, to be in Smewgy's form was to be in a measure ennobled."[11] Similarly, NYC Police Commissioner Bernard Kerik was profoundly influenced by his martial arts instructors and military leaders.

Sometimes a negative example can persuade a child to take up the opposite habit. Journalist and reformer Horace Greeley refused to touch alcohol or tobacco his entire life, probably because of his alcoholic father. He also had an incredible work ethic, and was frugal yet very generous to the poor because of the example set by his hard-working, pious mother.

Ideally though, a child should be surrounded by good examples rather than bad. The family can work together on conquering bad habits, a little at a time. If you have had a hard time correcting bad habits in the past, take heart, because each time you successfully change a behavior, no matter how small, the next time will be a little easier. Like a muscle, every time you exercise willpower it gets a little stronger.

I think the most common mistake parents make is leaving the child to his own efforts before a good habit has taken hold. It is hard when we are busy with so many other things, and we tend to forget—just like the child does. Then it is tempting to scold

176

him for not doing what he ought to have done. If the habit is really important to us, consistent supervision is more productive than scolding. It just takes time!

We all have habits, whether we are aware of them or not. Good or bad, they exert a powerful influence over our actions every day. If we want to make the most of our lives, the challenge is not to mindlessly obey our habits, but to form habits that obey us.

Remember This:

- Habits have power. Little at first, they grow in force to achieve big results.
- The habit of attention is particularly important for learning.
- Replace the unwanted behavior or thoughts immediately with the better choice, but don't lecture or pile on guilt in the process.
- One at a time, replace bad habits with good habits, and practice persistently for at least two to three months.
- Figure out which habits are most important, then break them into learnable "chunks."
- Keep it short, simple, direct, and above all—consistent! Think of the basketball coach. Demonstrate the right way to do something, then follow-up if necessary with short, task-based feedback, not judgment.
- Patience – Patience – Patience !!!

Chapter Thirteen
Nature's Gymnasium

"A child should have mudpies, grasshoppers, waterbugs, tadpoles, frogs, mud turtles, elderberries, wild strawberries, acorns, chestnuts, trees to climb, animals to pet, hay fields, pinecones, rocks to roll, sand, snakes, huckleberries and hornets—and any child who has been deprived of these has been deprived of the best part of his or her education."
—Luther Burbank

When Theodore Roosevelt became president, France sent over their ambassador to learn more about the famous "Rough Rider." The two made quite an impression on each other. Biographer William Roscoe Thayer told the story:

'Yesterday,' wrote Ambassador Jusserand, 'President Roosevelt invited me to take a promenade with him this afternoon at three. I arrived at the White House punctually, in afternoon dress and silk hat, as if we were to stroll in the Tuileries Garden or in the Champs Elysees. To my surprise, the President soon joined me in a tramping suit, with knickerbockers and thick boots, and soft felt hat, much worn. Two or three other gentlemen came, and we started off

179

at what seemed to me a breakneck pace, which soon brought us out of the city. On reaching the country, the President went pell-mell over the fields, following neither road nor path, always on, on, straight ahead! I was much winded, but I would not give in, nor ask him to slow up, because I had the honor of *La belle France* in my heart. At last we came to the bank of a stream, rather wide and too deep to be forded. I sighed relief, because I thought that now we had reached our goal and would rest a moment and catch our breath, before turning homeward. But judge of my horror when I saw the President unbutton his clothes and heard him say, 'We had better strip, so as not to wet our things in the Creek.' Then I, too, for the honor of France, removed my apparel, everything except my lavender kid gloves. The President cast an inquiring look at these as if they, too, must come off, but I quickly forestalled any remark by saying, 'With your permission, Mr. President, I will keep these on, otherwise it would be embarrassing if we should meet ladies.' And so we jumped into the water and swam across."[1]

Fortunately, Ambassador Jusserand was a good sport. He passed Roosevelt's impromptu manliness test and the two men became good friends afterwards. Roosevelt was a huge proponent of what he called "The Strenuous Life." He had no patience for weakness or cowardice and he had a great deal of respect for hard work and time spent outdoors doing daring things. Roosevelt knew anybody could do it because he himself had made the transformation. As a boy, he was small and frail with pale spindly legs. He suffered from frequent asthma attacks and spent too many frightening hours propped up on pillows trying to catch his breath. Because of his weakness, he was no match for other boys and had several mortifying experiences with bullies. He dreamed of emulating the tough brave soldiers and Western heroes in his books, but it wasn't until the age of fourteen that he decided to do something about it.

With the enthusiastic blessing of his father, Roosevelt decided to start training and conditioning his body. His father built a family gymnasium.

> *"I am only an average man but, by George, I work harder at it than the average man."*
>
> —Theodore Roosevelt

He began wrestling and boxing lessons. He ran, swam, rowed skiffs, rode horses, and tromped the hills. As he grew stronger, he went on extended backpacking, hunting, and climbing trips. He was the first to admit that he was not a natural athlete. It took him years to make much improvement and he never excelled at any of his sports, but he had fun and developed an amazing vitality that left an impression on everyone he met. Throughout his life, Roosevelt considered physical strength and health paramount to any endeavor. What good is it to dream great things without the strength to do them?

Roosevelt was not the only one to transform his own health. Photographer Ansel Adams was also small and frail, and he came down with frequent colds and flu, which he attributed to poor knowledge of diet at the time. He also claimed to have been hyperactive and emotionally fragile, prone to periods of weeping. The doctor prescribed a two-hour nap every afternoon in a darkened room, but Ansel claimed that this just made things worse because he craved the outdoors. He was very active and could not seem to find enough outlets for his energies. He adored being outside and spent every available moment exploring the sand dunes and rivers near his San Francisco home. At the age of fourteen, he convinced his father to take the family on vacation to Yosemite. The beauty and wildness of the Sierras were a revelation to Ansel. He was busy morning till night hiking, exploring, swimming, and taking photographs with his new Kodak Box Brownie camera, a gift from his father. He became friends with a retired geologist, dubbed Uncle Frank, who took the boy on extended hiking and camping trips. Ansel loved it so much that he returned every summer, exploring the mountains with Uncle Frank. Later, at the age of seventeen, he became seriously ill with the flu and was not recovering properly. Ansel begged to return to Yosemite, and within weeks he regained his color and energy. He would always credit the mountain's healing powers for his recovery.

Time Outside

Spending time outdoors was a consistent theme of the children I studied, even the ones who did not become naturalists. Author Margaret Atwood spent a great deal of time in the Canadian backwoods. General George Patton climbed trees and rode horses. Artist Andrew Wyeth played Robin Hood with friends in the forest. Composer Irving Berlin regularly swam the filthy and treacherous East River to Brooklyn. Alexander Graham Bell loved to roam the Scottish countryside with his brother. Walt Whitman spent hours daydreaming under the shade of apple trees. This is not even counting the children who grew up on farms, working outside and caring for animals.

> *"Never throughout history has a man who lived a life of ease left a name worth remembering."*
>
> —Theodore Roosevelt

I wonder how many of our modern kids spend this much time outside? It's a different world now. Very few families live on farms anymore, and those that live in the suburbs may only have a backyard to explore. We also have different expectations about supervision these days. Our culture has become more protective, more alert to strangers and potential dangers. From what I have read about history, I honestly don't think our communities are any more dangerous now than they used to be. It's just that we *hear* about bad things happening more in the media, and have responded by raising our standards of child care and protection.

I'm not saying this is a bad thing. But we need to be aware of what has been lost. In the past, kids were often turned loose to explore with only a few warnings about places to avoid. Nowadays, that would be considered irresponsible, and children are kept close by—meaning that if Mom or Dad doesn't want to go in the woods, neither will the child. The price for greater safety shouldn't mean kids ensconced inside with the television set.

It's a balancing act to be sure. Parents have to decide how much freedom to give their children based on the child's maturity level and the likely dangers of their environment. But regardless of supervision, kids need to get outside. They need exercise. You need exercise too. If you live in a city, take them on walks to a park or to an arboretum if you have one. Visit the country. Artist Beatrix Potter grew up in London where she was allowed to visit the Natural History Museum by herself. But her favorite times were summers spent in the Scottish countryside. This is where she really came alive, scouring the woods with her brother, collecting specimens and drawing.

Nature Walks

Spending time outdoors isn't just healthy for the body, it is a veritable feast for the senses and intellect. Scientific understanding is so much more than simply reading books about what someone else has learned. What about all the people who wrote the books in the first place? Someone somewhere *observed* the phenomenon first, then loved it enough to study and write a book about it. (Hint: when it's time to read, choose these books.) Biologists don't just sit inside reading other people's work; they

183

investigate, observe, test, and take notes. To be sure, lots of people already know what juniper smells like or where to find garter snakes, but why not let children discover those things for themselves? This is inquiry-based vs. fill-the-bucket style learning, and our national science educators would love to promote more of it.[2]

> *"I sincerely believe that for the child, and for the parent seeking to guide him, it is not half so important to know as to feel when introducing a young child to the natural world. If facts are the seeds that later produce knowledge and wisdom, then the emotions and the impressions of the senses are the fertile soil in which the seeds must grow. The years of early childhood are the time to prepare the soil."*
>
> —Rachel Carson, *A Sense of Wonder*

So what should we do? What does outdoor learning look like? Since studying nature and exploring wild places used to be very common in the Victorian era, it's worth looking at role models from this time. Theodore Roosevelt is one example; Beatrix Potter, John Burroughs, John Muir, Andrew Carnegie, Alexander Graham Bell, Thomas Edison, Douglas MacArthur, Walt Whitman, Robert Frost, and the Wright Brothers are others. In each case, the ample time these children spent outside was unstructured. There was no adult telling them what to do or teaching them, but very often the adult was called upon to answer questions. Thomas Edison was one of those who asked a hundred questions a day, and when his father could not answer, the boy would turn to him and ask, "Why *don't* you know?"[3]

Charlotte Mason's advice for parents and teachers matches this pattern. She believed young children should spend as much time as possible outside, and that the adults should stay in the background rather than run the show. In her book, *Home Education: Training and educating children under nine*, Charlotte Mason tells of a judicious mother who reported that her children were out of doors for one hour a day in the winter and two hours a day in the summer. Mason replied:

> That is well; but it is not enough. In the first place, do
> not send them; if it is anyway possible take them; for,
> although the children should be left much to them-
> selves, there is a great deal to be done and a great deal
> to be prevented during these long hours in the open
> air. And long hours they should be; not two, but four,
> five, or six hours they should have on every tolerably
> fine day, from April till October. 'Impossible!' says an
> over-wrought mother who sees her way to no more
> for her children than a daily hour or so on the pave-
> ments of the neighboring London squares. Let me
> repeat, that I venture to suggest, not what is practica-
> ble in any household, but what seems to me *absolutely
> best for the children*; and that, in the faith that mothers
> work wonders once they are convinced that wonders
> are demanded of them. [italics in the original][4]

Yes, you heard it right—Ms. Mason believed that you are capable of wonders for the sake of your children. She did not think
it unreasonable for a mother to take her children and a picnic
basket on a 20-minute bus ride to the country every single fair
day. And what is the mother supposed to do in the country all
day long? Mason describes it this way:

> Our wise mother, arrived, first sends the children to
> let off their spirits in a wild scamper, with cry; hal-
> loo, and hullabaloo, and any extravagance that comes
> into their young heads . . . As for the baby, he is in
> bliss: divested of his garments, he kicks and crawls,
> and clutches the grass, laughs soft baby laughter, and
> takes in his little knowledge of shapes and properties
> in his own wonderful fashion—clothed in a woolen

185

gown, long and loose, which is none the worse for the worst usage it may get.[5]

After the children wander back to mother, she sends them off on scouting missions to explore various areas and report back what they find. Or perhaps she gives them a specific task to discover which way is north, or find the tallest tree or the smallest rock. Notice that this is not meant to be a structured "lesson plan," merely suggestions for when the kids are asking for another challenge. Margaret Mead's grandmother knew of this tactic and often gave young Margaret a description of a certain plant then sent her out to the woods and fields to collect examples of say, the "mint family."

> *"When one tugs at a single thing in nature; he finds it attached to the rest of the world."*
>
> —John Muir

Thomas Edison also used this technique with his children. On Sunday afternoon nature walks, he would challenge his children to find varieties of every form of vegetation they could find, then match their cuttings with his at the end of the walk to find out who had the most. Edison usually won.

Another game Charlotte Mason suggested was "Picture Painting." The child looks carefully at a certain patch of landscape then closes his eyes and tries to recreate the picture in his mind. He then tells someone what he sees, with as much detail and nuance as possible.

After children have exhausted their excess energy, they should be encouraged to watch living creatures carefully—ants, spiders, worms, beetles, birds, fish—and learn what they can of their habits. When they are old enough, Mason advised that all children should have nature notebooks to record their observations and sketch what they see.

When observation becomes tiresome, Mason suggested that the children's daily French lesson should be given, but otherwise she warned mothers not to talk much overall. The mother should not get too much between the children and their own explorations. After a picnic lunch, older children might have energy left for noisy games while the younger children rest. But after a full day outside, all the children should be fully tuckered out when they arrive home.

The result of all this time outdoors isn't just healthy children, but healthy learning. They are learning to observe, pay attention, recall what they see, and make connections. Young children especially need to touch things, move around, and make noise. It is so hard to meet these needs indoors.

Adults have an unfortunate tendency to discount learning if it doesn't come from textbooks or workbooks—as if that were the only way to learn anything. As much as Charlotte Mason loved good books, she was wise enough to know that children learn through their hands and hearts as well. They *need* to form associations with the natural world around them.

Even as they get older, children can still do their "school" work outdoors or bring a book up into the branches of a tree. I often read aloud books to my kids on a large blanket spread under a maple tree. There they could wiggle and squirm to their heart's content, all while enjoying the story. My oldest son often could not resist acting out certain scenes from a story, such as Pagoo the hermit crab wriggling out of his outgrown shell or all the animals piling on Turtle's back in a Native American folktale.

> *"Come forth into the light of things.*
> *Let nature be your teacher."*
> —William Wordsworth

I had heard of Charlotte Mason's penchant for nature walks when my kids were little, and I tried to follow it, but somehow I missed the part about four to six hours a day outside. I'm not sure I would have done it, but I learned later how right she was.

Kids need a LOT more exercise than you may think. When my son Jesse used to act up, my husband frequently sent him outside to run around the house three times. This helped somewhat, but it was not until Jesse was older that I learned how much more exercise he needed. (Perhaps running around the house for three *hours* would have done the trick.) Park days, walks to the pond, and homeschool gym time were not nearly enough. That boy needed swim team, skateboarding, and neighborhood football games every day to really get worn out. And when he was worn out, he relaxed, he smiled, he sighed with contentment. My daughter was the same way. Her emotional state seemed directly connected with how many hours of sports or active play she participated in that day—the more the better. Perhaps if I had realized this sooner, I could have saved us all needless frustration and willingly sacrificed four to six hours of housework for the chance to read a book outside on a blanket.

Personal Power

I'm not the only one to find a connection between health and success. A healthy lifestyle usually tops the list of important habits success experts recommend. It's difficult to do our best if we have no energy or focus to devote to it. The most fundamental tool we have to accomplish our dreams is ourselves, and it is absolutely imperative that we take good care of that tool. Both Orison Swett Marden and Stephen R. Covey (author of *The 7 Habits of Highly Effective People*) called it "sharpening the saw." An intelligent woodsman spends the time to sharpen his saw before attempting to cut down a tree, because this helps him do the job more effectively.

Most of the successful people I studied didn't just exist, they gave thought and effort to their eating, hygiene, and exercise habits (except for the really obsessive types who could barely remember to get dressed in the morning). They either learned on their own or from their parents.

Models of Health

Once again, parents are the subjects of nonstop scrutiny from the time our children are born till the time they forget to call us once a week. We make it a lot easier for them to learn good habits if we model those habits first. Not only will it help your kids, but it will also help *you* to be more effective. Over time, you will feel better and have more energy to do the things you need to do. Just think of how fatigue or a headache or digestive problems can affect your whole day. It doesn't have to be that way. But in order to model the best habits you may need to undo some of the ones you grew up with. Take the time to learn about healthy habits—particularly nutrition. This is something young children can't do on their own. You buy (or grow) their food. No matter what breakfast cereal or snack food is advertised on TV, it is entirely up to you what lands in the pantry and on the dining table. You as a parent need to advocate and model a healthy lifestyle—it's not realistic to think you can slack off and still expect your kids to do better than you.

Being healthy doesn't just mean the absence of obvious sickness. It means feeling *good*, with energy and vitality to spare. Health has everything to do with how well we learn, our emotions, our relationships, and our attitude towards life. It is the

> *"Personal power is the aim of every sane ambition. We may not think about it in just that way, but whether we are bending our energies to make money or to write books, to paint pictures or to make machines, to win a position in the professional ranks or to build up a big business, to make a fortune or to serve society, whatever our immediate ambition, our real aim is to do more and to be more. Increase of ability, increase of strength, increase of power to accomplish our aim is what we are all after. There is no way of gaining this increase so effectively as the doing of everything that will perfect and preserve our health."*
>
> —Orison Swett Marden[6]

foundation of everything we do, and it deserves just as much attention as curriculum in your homeschool plans. In fact, if you are spending all your parental energy on curriculum and discipline matters at the expense of healthful habits such as exercise, lots of veggies, fresh air, sunshine, pure water, and clean living then you are making your job unnecessarily difficult.

Stephen Covey speaks of "sharpening the saw" as renewal. He teaches that we all need balanced renewal of our mental, physical, social/emotional, and spiritual energies to be most effective. Committing to regular renewal and self-improvement affects everything else we do. Our bodies become stronger. Our willpower becomes stronger. Our emotional and spiritual well-being grows stronger. It's worth it!

Remember This:

- A strenuous life full of hard work, exercise and time outside to do adventurous things will increase personal power.
- Young kids need plenty of unstructured, but supervised, time outdoors to explore and play. Bring a book to read, a picnic lunch, and a head full of ideas to challenge your kids when they ask for more. (See the Appendix for some great books on this.)
- Even if they cannot be outside, aim for four to six hours a day of active play, sports, or other exercise.
- Model healthy habits for your kids. Like any new habit, it may be hard at first to commit to time outdoors, regular exercise, or a healthier diet, but it will get easier as your willpower toughens up.

Chapter Fourteen
The Dreaded Screen Conundrum

"All television is educational television. The question is: what is it teaching?"

—Nicholas Johnson

Have you ever debated with your local homeschool group over the question of TV/computers/gaming? It's a contentious issue for sure. Some parents have banned television and computers from their homes, while others see no problem with letting kids watch all day. Most of us fall somewhere between, setting some sort of limits on screen time. But that still leaves us with the question: How much is too much? I would have liked to have drawn anecdotal conclusions from my study of famous homeschoolers, but most on my list grew up before the age of televisions, video games, and computers. So I have looked at other research for insight on this matter, as these new media are far too prevalent in our modern home environment to just ignore.

Like it or not, "screens" of all sizes are now part of the atmosphere our kids are growing up with, and for the purposes of this book, I want to explore their effect in three areas: self-education, creativity, and habits.

Self-Education

I don't think anyone would argue with the fact that we are living in an "information age." The Internet especially has revolutionized the way we generate and share information. Now we have classic and out-of-print books available for free online. We have the ability to search for information about anything, no matter how obscure, and actually *find* something.

I remember the first time my oldest son, then about six years old, wanted to find out about a topic that wasn't in any of our books—leeches. The Internet was still fairly new to me, but I typed "leeches" in the search box and was astounded by the results. Who knew there were so many types of leeches? Or how many people love leeches enough to create web sites about them?

Now we have YouTube videos to teach us how to brush our dog's teeth or crack open a coconut. We have Google maps to give us an actual aerial view of any place on Earth. We have online encyclopedias, foreign language dictionaries, magazines, newspapers, library databases, museum archives, virtual associations, and an ever-growing deposit of human knowledge to plunder.

Our problem now is not *lack* of information but deciding which information is correct or worthy of our time. Unlike Thomas Edison who had to take a train to Detroit in order to join a modest library, we can have the greatest library in the world delivered to our laptops 24 hours a day. Self-directed education has never been easier. Children just need a little guidance on safety and discernment while using the Internet.

The Internet also makes finding mentors, teachers, and kindred spirits easier than ever. We can search community listings for volunteer opportunities, cultural events, or Meetup groups. We can find tutors and job listings on Craigslist or field trips with the local hiking club, along with support groups for everything from homeschooling to autism.

As long as kids are thoroughly briefed—and supervised if necessary—on the safety and privacy protocols for the Internet, it can be a fabulous resource.

Creativity

The visual images delivered via television and computer screens may have another role besides self-education—stimulation of creative thought. Thomas G. West, author of *Thinking Like Einstein* and *The Mind's Eye*, makes a compelling case for the relationship between visual media, particularly computer graphics, and right-brained thought processes. He explains that humans are naturally visual, but with the advent of pervasive literacy we moved away from our visual-spatial roots in favor of a word-centered culture. West does not question the tremendous value of books, though, only the degree to which they have supplanted other forms of thinking. He writes:

> Some wonder whether it is really useful or even possible to think in pictures. Indeed, if you want to think clearly and precisely about something, they ask, doesn't it have to be done in words? Isn't visualization just a lot of pretty pictures, as they say, smoothed and textured and colored to be pleasing—useful for laypersons perhaps but never for hard-headed, serious professionals? These prejudices have long been evident in Western culture—varying from field to field, more or less—for decades or for hundreds of years. From ancient times, often the highest prestige has been reserved for occupations associated with writ-

193

ten language and the book—for the small elite who had an academic education and proximity to power, the priests and the clerks who had control of the technology of writing and the book.

But, as we have been saying, all this seems likely to change in fundamental ways. The enduring prestige of the written word, we can now see, is wrapped up in the power of writing and reading as a technology. This technology changed forever the transitory and ephemeral nature of ordinary speech and the long-standing oral tradition. In a similar fashion, I expect the new technology of computer graphics and data visualization to deeply transform our own culture, gradually shifting from a world based largely on words to one where images will have a much more important role: a new world where the real action will be in learning to develop deep and sophisticated understandings of complex systems by internalizing complex, moving three-dimensional images—that is, by building models in the mind.[1]

West gives many examples in his books of how traditional academic approaches to science, business, and engineering can suffer from a myopic inability to solve problems. It is often the truly visual thinkers who are able to detect the pattern behind mounds of data. Some of our greatest scientists—Einstein, Faraday, Maxwell, Feynman, Tesla—were highly visual. They saw, felt, and *imagined* forces that eluded others.

This unique ability will become even more important as more mundane skills are taken over by computers. Just as machines have replaced many traditional labor jobs, computers have already replaced many clerical jobs—and will continue to do so. But there are still limitations to what a computer can do.

Just think of that anti-spam feature on many websites where the webmaster asks you to enter the weirdly shaped word "shown in the box below." This is to make sure you are a human and not a program. Humans are very good at seeing patterns and meaning. Perhaps that is why we have taken this skill for granted, relegating it to a less important status than reading, writing, and arithmetic.

In *Thinking Like Einstein*, West writes:

> Well-intended but misguided efforts toward educational reform place too much emphasis on, as I have mentioned in previous chapters, what are really the skills of a medieval clerk: reading, writing, counting, and memorizing texts. In contrast, it seems that what we should now be focusing on are the skills that will be important in the lives of the children of today—not the skills that were important for our grandparents. And these are likely to be the skills of a Renaissance visual thinker like Leonardo da Vinci, using new visualization technologies to understand patterns in the world largely using the rapid and integrative visual-spatial intelligence—perhaps learning in the near future, as a culture, to employ the other side of our brain, after centuries of relative disuse.[2]

West isn't just advocating computer technologies, however. He points out the importance of all the so-called right-brained activities: drawing, sculpting, music, imagination, hands-on learning. Knowing how to use computer animation software does not make someone an artist. They must learn to be an artist first, with all the rigorous training and practice that term implies. The computer is only a tool to model what the human mind perceives.

What all this means for screen time, is that visual media

should not be vilified just because it is not a book—pictures instead of words. Books are wonderful, indispensable tools for thinking and learning; but computers, movies, television, and yes—even video games—have a lot to offer too. These technologies are unleashing a torrent of innovation that most companies can barely keep up with.

In his book, *Geeks: How Two Lost Boys Rode the Internet out of Idaho*, Jon Katz tells the story of Jesse Dailey and Eric Twilegar struggling (and succeeding) to make something of themselves in a world that doesn't understand them. As Katz followed their progress, he collected observations from other idiosyncratic kids, routinely ostracized or hazed in school. He makes the point that technology, especially the Internet, is transforming their lives, giving them a social and intellectual outlet long-denied by traditional society. In fact, it is giving them an advantage. The world *depends* on technology geeks now. Without them, industry and government would grind to a halt—sweet revenge for all the teasing and scorn heaped upon them in high school. Machines, robots, the Internet, and computer software that does everything from databases to 3-D modeling have changed the cultural landscape. We now have more sophisticated equipment for scientific research, medicine, entertainment, manufacturing, and defense. Aside from the technical expertise needed to run all these things, we need great minds to show us what we can *do* with all these inventions—and what these inventions do to us.

> *"When we survey examples of highly successful visual thinkers and dyslexics, we can see that they have many strengths that are often not properly recognized in school or university—but are recognized in work and in life. We need to find ways of seeing and developing the gifts and talents hidden under the difficulties. Successful visual thinkers and dyslexics succeed by following their substantial gifts, not by focusing on their difficulties."*[3]
> —Thomas G. West

196

Dyslexia

In his books, Thomas G. West presents the case that many of our most gifted visual thinkers also had reading, mathematical, or verbal difficulties. Michael Faraday is widely recognized as a brilliant scientist, particularly in the fields of electricity and magnetism. But he was not able to convey his discoveries in the traditional mathematical form expected by his peers. It took another visual thinker, James Clerk Maxwell, to translate Faraday's discoveries into mathematical equations. Maxwell was able to understand Faraday's visual world of images, models, and diagrams along with the relevant mathematics—although he himself had severe, lifelong speech problems.

Albert Einstein is notorious for his late development of speech. His sister Maja also reported that he was slow to calculate math problems and made frequent errors despite a deep understanding of the underlying principles.

Craig McCaw, one of the pioneers of the cell phone industry, is dyslexic, but this may have worked to his advantage. Because of his difficulty reading, he avoids lengthy documents and concentrates instead on thinking. He has a unique ability to think about problems from different perspectives and angles, which McCaw credits for his success in business. This ability allowed him to see the great potential in wireless communications before others did.[4]

People who gravitate towards visual-spatial careers in architecture, computer graphics, medical surgery, art, design, and engineering very often have some degree of dyslexia. Indeed, dyslexia is sometimes referred to as the "MIT Disease."

If you have a child who you suspect has unusual verbal or reading difficulties, there are programs available to help diagnose the problem and teach accordingly. But it is important to realize that such differences do not make a child any less intelligent. Focus on your children's strengths even while helping them mitigate their weaknesses.

What we need are creative people who can think outside traditional constraints and march to their own inner drumbeat—otherwise known as geeks. Katz, a writer for *Rolling Stone* and *Wired* magazines, interviewed the founder of *Wired*, Louis Rossetto, who said:

The new cultural class has no physical demands or restrictions. There are music geeks and dance geeks. Geekdom is evolving. Anybody who is obsessed with a topic and becomes completely one with it . . . whether it's computers, music, or art—geeks come into that. Geeks is sometimes about technology but mostly, it's about brains, and about being resented for being smart. . . . [geeks] revel in redefining what's possible, they are inherently revolutionaries. They live to hallucinate new visions, to invent the next big thing, to prove the smug adherents of the status quo wrong. For the longest time, they were unappreciated, servants to bureaucrat and politicians in whatever organization they were part of, a benign cult relegated to the margins of social respectability. But in a world where the human mind is the most precious node on the planet's nervous system, pure meritocracy is not only possible and desirable, but inevitable.[5]

If the definition of a geek is someone who is passionate and smart (but temporarily ostracized for being different), than let's make more of them! Then creative difference will become the norm and the term "geek" will become obsolete. But to make more geeks, we need to provide them with their choice of intellectual fodder. Creativity and passion thrive on freedom—including the freedom to play a video game or watch a television program.

The thing to remember is that just as some books are junk, some visual media (quite a bit actually) is junk. Kids should know this and we can teach them to be conscious consumers. Talk to your kids about why they want to watch something. They may have reasons that you will not understand at first. Janna Levin, professor of physics and astronomy at Columbia University, grew up watching hours of *Star Trek* and other sci-fi television.[6] Screenwriter/Director Quentin Tarantino was obsessed with watching "B" movies. NYC Police Commissioner Bernard Kerik was inspired by TV shows like the *Green Hornet* and various police dramas. We can't assume which shows would be more worthwhile than others, but we should eliminate the ones that are clearly inappropriate.

Also, don't make the mistake of thinking that a family board/card game is better than a family (multi-player) video console game just because it is more traditional. The new format may be trickier (for adults) to master, but there are a lot of creative, challenging, puzzle-solving video games available that are fun for family and friends to play together.

Habits

Now that I've drummed up the value of visual media for self-education and creativity, it's time to take it down a notch.

I believe that television, DVDs, computers, and video games can be worthwhile as long as they are used with deliberation and thought. The problem arises when these things interfere with otherwise good habits. If we are watching a certain program because it is fascinating, that's OK. But if we are simply surfing through cable channels and websites because we are too lazy to do anything else, that's different.

Remember that the secret to developing self-discipline is doing things that are hard. Watching television is notoriously easy. Playing computer or video games is more challenging but potentially addictive. Ask yourself if you and your family are using visual media intentionally as a resource—or as a mindless habit.

Habits, either good or bad, shape us. How we spend our days is, of course, how we spend our lives. So we need to give it thought and decide how best to use the time that is given us.

Older children can think for themselves on this too. Have conversations about what you like and don't like, and how computers and video fit in to your life plans. If you feel that your child is truly addicted to a game and unable to limit playing on his own, it might be appropriate to step in and break the cycle. But it is always better for a kid to set limits for himself first. If you set the limits it is *your d*iscipline, if he sets the limits it becomes *self*-discipline.

I do think visual media has a valid place in modern society, but not as a time-filler. Science fiction author Ursula K. Leguin explains the trade-off well: "There was no TV then; we turned on the radio once a day to get the war news. Those summers of solitude and silence, a teenager wandering the hills on my own, no company, 'nothing to do,' were very important to me. I think I started making my soul then."[7]

Everybody needs empty time to process the barrage of information and noise we meet every day. Otherwise the days rush by in a blur without truly experiencing them. This is especially true for children under the age of eight or nine.

During this stage of development, young children need to be physically doing things—not sitting in front of a TV (or even at a desk with a workbook). They should be spending all day every day outside if possible; running around, playing games, investigating, climbing, touching. Children are very tactile—just look at any Montessori classroom or children's museum. They love to pour, paint, cut, stack, open, close, zip, button, match, pet, squeeze, and push buttons. But kids aren't doing these things when they are watching cartoons.

The authors of *The Creative Spirit* made a good point about how modern children get a great deal of information through TV but don't actually do as much hands-on stuff.

In a real sense, children know more but understand

less. The hands-on experience children had in earlier times with agriculture and crafts made clear to them that life is a process of doing, and that a process has a beginning, a middle, and an end. Through its quick succession of images and compression of time, television destroys this sense of process, conveying the illusion that things just 'happen.'[8]

It is very tempting to plop your little ones in front of a Disney movie just so you can have a rest or make dinner in peace. Believe me—I know. I have experimented with various amounts of screen time when my kids were little and always found that the short-term gains of peace and quiet didn't make up for the longer-term behavior problems. My kids loved to watch animated movies but they always seemed cranky afterwards. Once we cut movies down to twice a week, their mood and behavior improved dramatically. Try it and see what happens.

Another way to look at the issue of young children and screen time is what it means for you the parent. Using the television as a babysitter makes your life temporarily easier, but less rewarding overall. Bringing your kids outside to wear them out with nature walks, play-dates at the park, working in the garden, or sports involves more time and effort, but it is more rewarding. Your kids will be healthier, happier, and ready to go to bed early. You will have a messier house, but better relationships with your kids—and much better memories.

Later, as children get older, it may be appropriate for them to have more time on "screens" as their interests take focus. Let media be a tool for research, entertainment, and self-expression. Talk about what they see. Do they know which sources are more credible, and how to evaluate advertising and propaganda? Just teach your kids to recognize the difference between *using* the media as a tool and being *used by* the media as a fool.

Remember This:

- New visual media technologies, particularly the Internet, have revolutionized self-education. Learn to make the most of it!
- Books are wonderful, irreplaceable tools for understanding our world. But words are not inherently better than pictures. Pictures (or video) can stimulate creative thinking.
- Choose your media carefully, just like you would choose a book.
- Don't watch a program simply because you are bored—watch when it is fascinating.
- Kids under the age of eight or so should not be sitting in front of a screen—maybe an *occasional* movie or special show. Otherwise they should be outside, playing or doing something hands-on.
- If you really need to distract your little ones, try listening to children's music or a book-on-CD. They can still wiggle around, build with blocks, or do other things while listening!
- Let older kids plan their screen consumption, but if they are addicted, you need to step in and help.

Chapter Fifteen
Putting it All Together

"That which we are, we are all the while teaching, not voluntarily,
but involuntarily."
—Ralph Waldo Emerson

The famous homeschoolers I read about were not geniuses. They were not necessarily rich or lucky or special in any way. But they had two things in common:

Passion and Determination

I am convinced that the root of passion is simply the freedom to find it. The reason some of us never find our passion is because we can not hear ourselves over the din of other people telling us what to do and what to learn. This is especially true for children who are so malleable and trusting. Maybe that is why so many creative originals were feisty and independent as youngsters—they were the ones strong enough to follow their inclinations.

Freedom to find one's passion also implies the freedom to direct one's own education. This is not to say that the parent is not involved—far from it. A loving parent must be a child's first mentor and support system. We are their ticket to the world. They need our help to visit places, meet people, and find the best resources/books/lessons to pursue their interests. They need our patience while they figure out who they want to be. They need time, space, and a rich atmosphere of authentic experience.

Once a youth finds his or her passion, though, it takes determination to do something with it. Achievement doesn't just happen. Some people might be born with more determination than others, but there are things we can do to help our kids develop this critical skill. Like a muscle, determination can be exercised and built up over time. To do this, children must be given a chance to make decisions and experience consequences—whether good or bad. They must be given a chance to do real, meaningful work which results in real achievement, whether it is a paycheck, a well-built chicken coop, a winning soccer season, or simply the satisfaction of a job well done. No fake work and no fake achievement! They can be supported when they show initiative, but parents shouldn't take over the project.

> *"Just as eating against one's will is injurious to health, so studying without a liking for it spoils the memory, and it retains nothing it takes in."*
>
> —Leonardo Da Vinci

Some critics may say that self-directed education is a cop-out; that it is way too easy for kids and negligent of parents. My response is that it is really the only way anyone learns anything. You can make a child fill out a worksheet or take a test, but you can't make him really learn or remember the material. That's up to the child. Learning is an inherently personal pursuit—unlike work. It's true that kids who diligently do their homework and study hard are building self-discipline. But unless they are really interested in the material, or have made up their minds to learn it, it will soon be forgotten after the test. They are not necessarily learning anything, just working for the grade.

I'd say it is far better to learn what is meaningful *and* do work that is meaningful. That means letting the student direct her own education, but at the same time, expect her to do plenty of work as part of the household and community. The idea is not a life of leisure, but a life of passion and determination.

Leading the Way

This is where you come in. For both passion and determination, it is critical for parents to lead the way. Our positive attitude towards learning and work will teach kids more than any curriculum.

How are *your* habits? What are *you* learning? What is *your* passion?

We are the role models, whether we like it or not. Don't worry—it's OK if you're not perfect. But it's important to try. Take stock of your own shortcomings and resolve to do better—starting with attitude. A positive mental attitude makes everything else so much easier, because your mind will think anything is possible. Be grateful for your blessings and confident that things will turn out just fine.

I once attended a presentation by the poet Maya Angelou and she said something intriguing that puzzled me for years. She believed that everyone should memorize at least one poem, because poetry "gives you backbone." She explained that when times are tough, it is important to have those luminous words of wisdom tucked in the back of your head. I was doubtful at first that any poem could be that important, but now I understand what she meant. It is comforting to know that we are not alone. Someone, somewhere has felt like this before, and knowing this can give us hope. That's what Maya Angelou meant by "backbone" — hope. I think that is also the basis for a positive mental attitude. It makes anything bearable and everything possible.

Once you have your head in the right place, then it's time to accomplish things. Kids don't need to set long-term goals, but adults should. If you haven't already, spend some introspective time deciding on goals for yourself and perhaps your family. Whole books have been written on this so I will not attempt to guide you through it here, but I have included a list of resources in the Appendix.

> *"Our goals can only be reached through a vehicle of a plan,*
> *in which we must fervently believe,*
> *and upon which we must vigorously act.*
> *There is no other route to success."*
>
> —Pablo Picasso

If this is a book about homeschooling, why am I talking about self-improvement and setting goals for parents? Because parents are the role models. Effective homeschooling is not about pushing a child to achieve our idea of success. Our ideas may not match his or her own innate genius. The best we parents can do is demonstrate successful habits while giving our kids the freedom to choose their own path. Though homeschooling (and parenting) takes a lot of thought and energy, you should not devote all of it to your kids. Take the time to further your own education, learn new things, read, work part-time, or take up a hobby.

Perhaps you are already a super-achiever. I think many homeschooling parents are. But in this case it is important not to overwhelm your child with pressure to succeed and "be like you." They may be nothing like you at all. Love your children just the way they are, and support their unique creative quests while pursuing your own.

Tim White, professor in the Laboratory for Human Evolutionary Studies of the University of California, described his childhood growing up in the mountains:

> So what made [me] choose a life in science? It was
> the freedom. My parents never pushed me in any ca-
> reer direction. For this freedom I cannot thank them
> enough. I inherited their skepticism (they were dead
> set against religious orthodoxy), their fascination with
> things historical and natural, their curiosity. The op-
> portunity for a kid to grow up in the mountains came
> only because my parents were young and willing to
> take a risk, to seek a better and more interesting life.
> I was the luckiest kid in the world, a privileged pas-
> senger along for the ride of his life.[1]

Notice in this passage that it was the parents who were seeking a better and more interesting life. They were pursuing their
own passions and bringing their son "along for the ride." They
didn't focus all of their attention and energy on him, nor pressure him into any particular career. It may seem obvious, but we
should not live through our kids. If we really want to take over
the world, we shall have to do it ourselves.

What do I do then?

For Children under the Age of Ten — Heart and Hands

Children this age are natural explorers—asking questions,
looking under rocks, touching everything, learning how to move
and how to do the things older people do. They need time and
space to do all these things—and a generous amount of parental
patience. Take them places, answer questions, let them try stuff.
If they want to know more about trains or dinosaurs or how animals lay eggs, find a book from the library that will answer their
questions. If they want to learn how to read, then by all means
teach them—but don't push it.

Remember whenever you are tempted to pull out a work-book, that workbooks were invented by adults who want something to measure—some way to test what a child knows about colors or shapes or letters or whatever. But those paltry symbols of instruction are nothing compared to what children are learning all by themselves just by watching, listening, and exploring on their own. The problem is that this work is invisible and hard to measure. What adults might see as idle play is actually the child's way of building sensory and physical coordination, along with imagination and problem-solving. Just because it doesn't look like school doesn't mean it isn't real learning.

Some left-brained type kids may enjoy workbooks. They find them very satisfying. My second son was like that. He wanted to try some of those colorful mass-market type workbooks, so I bought a couple for him. But he didn't often use them the way they were intended. Instead he used the empty space at the top of the page to copy words from the instructions. Later, he skipped through the book only doing the puzzles, word searches, and mazes. From then on, I only bought him puzzle books and he was happy.

Relying on self-education eliminates the problem of figuring out your child's learning style because your child will naturally want to learn things the way that makes sense for him. All you need to do is pay attention.

Pay attention to what your kids are craving (no, not sugar). What do they love to do? Play with balls? Look for centipedes? Build tent forts? Whatever it is, try to accommodate them. Child-led learning may sound easier for parents, but it's definitely not! It takes a lot of time and energy to give a child what they really need. Nature walks, playing games, reading aloud, and making things take far more effort than plunking a child down at the kitchen table to do schoolwork—there's just less fighting involved.

When I was experimenting with "unschooling" I made the mistake of thinking that every day must be unstructured. In the morning I would ask the kids what they wanted to do and they would invariably ask to make something or do a science experiment. My oldest would flip through one of our many project books and find one that looked enticing but it always seemed like I was missing some crucial component (empty 2 liter bottle, baby food jar, large balloon, pickling lime, etc.). This is when I learned that it is OK to ask my kids to plan ahead. Self-education doesn't have to mean *spontaneous*. I'm not a vending machine after all. So from then on, I asked the kid to select activities and craft projects ahead of time and mark the pages with sticky notes so I could collect the materials beforehand.

I also found that my kids usually *liked* it when I planned or suggested an activity, like putting on a puppet show or taking a class on survival skills, because they had never heard of such things before. But if I suggested something boring, they were free to decline or choose something else.

> *Daniel C. Dennett, a philosophy professor, author, and director of the Center for Cognitive Studies at Tufts University, used the word "renaissance" to describe his childhood and youth. He thoroughly enjoyed jumping from topic to topic: engineering, jazz, painting, sculpture, philosophy, teaching, science. "As a result, I'm an autodidact – or, more properly, the beneficiary of hundreds of hours of informal tutorials on all the fields that interest me, from some of the world's leading scientists. Lucky me. But I wasn't a kid when I fell in love with science. I just felt like one."[2]*

My rule of thumb for homeschooling young children is that they learn best through their heart and hands. By "hands" I mean hands-on play, exploration, and manipulation. By "heart" I mean love and care, but also emotion—accessed through story-telling. All people crave stories, but especially children. This is one of the primary differences between "living" books and insipid made-tosell-market books. A well-crafted story has a little piece of the author's soul mixed in. The characters feel true and we care about what happens to them. Stories, whether narrated or read aloud, somehow satisfy a deep inner urge to understand ourselves and the world around us. Kids *need* this.

If you have a child who bristles at sitting down to hear a story, consider that the problem may be the sitting-down part. Contrary to what your third grade teacher may have told you, children do not need to hold still to listen. In fact, many children are unable to listen unless they are free to move. The other problem may be attention span. Start with very short 10-minute segments, and then as their attention span grows, gradually extend their reading time. This means that you may have to have separate reading times for different children. One child may be satisfied after only ten minutes while another child will beg for "just one more chapter."

Another tactic for reluctant listeners is to choose a different type of story. Children's librarians are wonderful resources for finding just the right books for your child. They will know about wonderful authors you may have never heard about. You could also try making up stories (or re-telling true stories) featuring your child as main character. Who could resist that?

Record Keeping for the Younger Years

One problem with choosing the "heart and hands" curriculum over a traditional school curriculum is the pressure you may receive from concerned relatives or the local school administrators. Depending on which state (or country) you live in, there may be onerous requirements for curriculum, attendance, and testing. You should be aware of the regulations. Don't ignore them, particularly as your child gets older because some state colleges will check on your compliance prior to admission.

The thing is, kids who pursue their own interests learn an awful lot. But not all of it is planned out in advance or dictated by a textbook. The way to prove what kids have learned is first journaling and scrapbooking, and then turning those into official looking portfolios should your local government require it.

Here's one method I recommend: Keep a small journal or planner with you during the day and make notes of what the kids do, funny things they say, or questions they ask. This will also give you something to do while waiting at ballet class or soccer practice. Do this every day!

Also keep a camera handy to take pictures of them building forts, practicing piano, playing with friends, reading (this especially appeals to worried grandparents), going on field trips, etc. Remember to take pictures of hard-to-store projects your kids have completed, like clay sculptures, cardboard armor, giant paintings, model airplanes, and sunflower gardens.

Next, create a file on your computer with a list of all the subjects required by your local regulations. Once a quarter, go through your journals and fill in the activities or books your kids completed under the appropriate subjects. You don't need lots of detail here—just a simple one-line entry with a date should do:

- "Oct. 19 – Field trip Nature Center, learned about migrating birds" would be entered under the science category.
- "Mar. 2 – Played with pattern blocks" would be entered under the math category.

You get the idea. Also keep a list of books read, regardless of subject matter. You'll be amazed how much stuff you do over the course of a year!

Along with written records, keep a file folder for each child for each year (filing cabinets are a homeschoolers best friend). This is where you keep their artwork, copies of written work, photos of 3-D projects and any paperwork about classes taken. If your child is especially prolific, there is no need to keep everything. If you can't decide what to keep, put it all in the folder and then at the end of the year throw away the obvious chaff.

> "The years teach much which the days never know."
>
> —Ralph Waldo Emerson

If you have time (don't laugh) at the end of a school year, try making a scrapbook with a large three-ring binder. Include all those pictures you took (along with appropriate journal notes), computer records, and samples of your child's best work.

The reason for doing all this is to prove to yourself and any possible skeptics that your child is indeed learning and growing without any government assistance or curriculum-in-a-box.

We often get so caught up in the rush of daily life that we don't remember the details. By writing it down and taking pictures, we can see how small things add up to big accomplishments. It also helps us remember what our kids were like. You think you will remember that funny thing they said or the games they played, but as new behavior replaces old behavior, your memories tend to be replaced as well.

Older Kids and Teens

As your kids get older, their ability to pre-plan their own education will become sharper. I won't mention any magic age when this will happen because it will be different for every child. Up to this point they will have been exploring all the many things that interest them and you will have been taking them places and introducing them to new people and activities. Eventually they will begin to think about their future and want to know about the possibilities. They will want to get more serious.

This is the time to sit down with them and do some research

on career and college requirements. If they want to go to college, then they will probably have to take a standardized test. Check out books from the library to show them what is on those tests. Then, together, make a plan for their teen years. What subjects will they study and when? Is there any class or training they need to take from someone else?

Most colleges have similar requirements for high school courses, but homeschoolers still have some flexibility with fulfilling those requirements. If your student wants to be a fashion designer, there is no reason why her world history course couldn't revolve around fashion. For English, she could read biographies of famous designers and write research papers on various aspects of design. She could start her own sewing business, and in the process learn business math, marketing, and time management. There may still be some required courses, like Algebra II and Chemistry, that don't fit her interests; but if a preferred college requires them, she will be mature enough to know that she must complete them anyway.

In this case it is nice to have a variety of curriculum products to choose from. This is one of the many great things about homeschooling—you're not stuck with the textbook that some school board committee selected for every subject. You get to choose what to use, and there are SO many great curriculum products on the market right now—unit studies, math software, online schools, great book lists and writing programs. It's wonderful to have more to choose from but also tough to decide. This is where you will have to do some digging—read reviews, talk to other homeschoolers and try to sample products before you buy. But above all else, let your student decide which ones seem right for her.

> *"When natural inclination develops into a passionate desire, one advances towards his goal in seven-league boots."*
> —Nikola Tesla

Record Keeping for Older Kids and Teens

Once you and your student have selected curriculum material, it helps to set reasonable deadlines for getting through it all (or whatever portion you choose to complete). This is good practice for breaking a large project into smaller tasks. At this point, I highly recommend using a good homeschool record-keeping program, either on software or paper. I like using software because it allows you to print out different records for different purposes. If your child plans to attend college, you will need to prepare a high school transcript for them, and good records are a must! I don't mean to intimidate you. It's not hard. Just find a system you like, learn how to use it, and be diligent about keeping track of completed work.

A side benefit of this is that your teen can still be responsible for her own education. If you have worked together to plan out courses and lesson plans in advance, then it is not *you* telling her what to do each week, it is the plan. I don't think it is necessary to have a detailed daily schedule (unless your teen really likes schedules). Usually a weekly to-do list is sufficient for your kids to check on Monday and complete as they see fit. Then on Friday, open up your record-keeping program and have your kids check off completed lessons, list the books they've read, and perhaps write a journal entry for the week. It is very satisfying to check off completed assignments and know that you're making progress toward a goal. On the other hand, if your student didn't finish her work for the week, it will be easier for her to see the negative consequences of a list that doesn't get any shorter!

"Have regular hours for work and play; make each day both useful and pleasant, and prove that you understand the worth of time by employing it well. Then youth will be delightful, old age will bring few regrets, and life will become a beautiful success."

—Louisa May Alcott

If your student has no interest in college and wants to pursue a trade or entrepreneurial venture, there is much less pressure to study subjects your child has no interest in. But she should still make a plan, and you should still help her keep good records. For one thing, your local homeschool regulations may require some proof of progress. Also, good records will come in handy in case she changes her mind about college or needs to create a resume.

> *"When we look back, the only things we cherish are those which in some way met our original want; the desire which formed in us in early youth, undirected, and of its own accord."*
>
> —Willa Cather

Growing Independence

In addition to "school" work, it is vitally important for your teens to get out of the house. This is the age when they need to find mentors/coaches/teachers for their particular interests. If they haven't yet zeroed in on any particular interest, continue to take them places and introduce them to new people and activities, but honor their preferences. If you thought they may like the local drama club, but they hate it, don't force them to continue. That's not fair to the teacher or the other students. If they generally like the club, but have a few bad days or problems with one of their peers, just listen to them and ask what they are going to do. Don't solve their problems for them (unless it is clearly a situation calling for adult intervention).

Allowing your students to own their decisions and problems is terrific practice for self-discipline, especially if they make mistakes! The best thing you can do is provide unconditional love and support. This means listening, not lecturing. This means that your child will never disappoint you, no matter what he does in life, because he is wonderful.

But just because he is wonderful is no reason to do his laundry. Teens are extremely capable and should be treated as such. They can and should support household maintenance, or have a job or volunteer work outside the home.

Confidence comes from doing real, possibly scary things—learning to use public transportation, meeting strangers, starting a business. Outdoor activities (with proper instruction first) such as backpacking, surfing, rock-climbing, and boating are great for building confidence. No matter what age we are, facing challenging situations will make us stronger—but not with helicopter parents hovering nearby.

Atmosphere

The other part of your homeschooling job is giving thought to the type of atmosphere your family lives in. The roots of passion and determination grow best in a rich, authentic atmosphere. It doesn't have to be fancy. It doesn't matter if you live in the city or the country or the suburbs or on a boat. Every family and community offers some unique combination of experiences to a growing child, but underlying all of it is the chance to meet interesting people, have conversations, read good books, play outside, do real work, and enjoy good health.

Consider eliminating screen time for kids under the age of seven. Then, with deliberation, gradually add in high quality movies, video/computer games, and Internet access as the kids get older.

> *"Feelings of worth can flourish only in an atmosphere where individual differences are appreciated, mistakes are tolerated, communication is open, and rules are flexible - the kind of atmosphere that is found in a nurturing family."*
>
> —Virginia Satir

No matter how humble your home, it should reflect your own love of learning. Whether it's music or stock market trading or training for a new career, keep learning, and the kids will catch your enthusiasm. They will know that learning isn't just something that happens at school or before the age of eighteen. Constant learning is crucial to success, no matter what your age. Of all the habits you will inevitably pass on to your kids, make sure a love of learning is one of them.

Conclusion

I wish I had done this research when my kids were younger. I would have done a few things differently in my own home school. But part of what I have learned has come from experience too. My Jesse never did learn to love math, but he did learn it. After years of math games, manipulatives, and hands-on activities, Jesse decided at the age of twelve that he ought to catch up to what the kids in school were doing. So we picked out a textbook and he buckled down to learn the material. It took some trial and error to figure out what worked best for him, but at least we weren't fighting anymore. He didn't enjoy math but he knew that he wanted to go to college, and thus needed to take the SAT test, so he worked hard (and ultimately did very well on the test).

We can't predict how our kids will turn out. I still don't know how Jesse or my other kids will turn out. Just like Steve Jobs explained in his commencement speech at Stanford, it's easier to "connect the dots backwards" to see how our various experiences lead to future achievement. But I really believe every child has a unique gift to offer the world, if they are only given a chance to develop both their passion and willpower. Self-education offers both.

Of all the great people who have lived and left the world a better place, most created their own success through sheer determination and pluck, not genius. They followed their passion, learned everything they could, sought mentors, worked hard, and imagined something that had never been done before. Nobody becomes a legend simply for high test scores or graduation from a prestigious college. Measurement by other people's standards only means more of the same. The idea is to bring forth the best that is in you, which may be something nobody has ever seen before. Our kids should do this too. We each have all the genius we need to live an extraordinary life.

Appendix
Helpful Resources

Listed in this Appendix are some of the books I've used and enjoyed over the years. For more resources on specific topics such as history, record-keeping, and science, please see my web site: www.legendarylearningnow.com

This is just a tiny sample of resources available for home-schoolers. There are always new and wonderful books, curriculum products, games and web sites being created. It's impossible to keep up with everything, but that's a good thing! There's never been a better time to craft your own education.

General Homeschooling

Albert, David. *Homeschooling and the Voyage of Self-discovery : A Journey of Original Seeking.* Monroe Me.: Common Courage Press, 2003.

Colfax, David. *Homeschooling for Excellence.* Warner Books ed. New York NY: Warner Books, 1988.

DeMille, Oliver. *A Thomas Jefferson Education : Teaching a Generation of Leaders for the Twenty-first Century.* 1st ed. [Cedar City Utah?]: TJEdOnline, 2009.

———, Rachel DeMille, and Diann Jeppson. *A Thomas Jefferson Education Home Companion.* Cedar City UT: George

Wythe College Press, 2006.

Dennis, Jeanne. *Homeschooling High School : Planning Ahead for College Admission*. 2nd ed. Lynwood WA: Emerald Books, 2004.

Gatto, John Taylor. *Dumbing Us Down: The Hidden Curriculum of Compulsory Schooling*. 2nd ed. Gabriola Island, BC: New Society Publishers, 2002.

Griffith, Mary. *The Unschooling Handbook : How to Use the Whole World as your Child's Classroom*. Rocklin CA: Prima Pub., 1998.

Holt, John. *Instead of Education : Ways to Help People do Things Better*. 1st ed. Boulder CO: Sentient Publications, 2004.

————. *Learning All the Time*. Reading Mass.: Addison-Wesley, 1989.

Kealoha, Anna. *Trust the Children : A Manual and Activity Guide for Homeschooling and Alternative Learning*. Berkeley Calif.: Celestial Arts, 1995.

Llewellyn, Grace. *The Teenage Liberation Handbook : How to Quit School and Get a Real Life and Education*. Eugene Or.: Lowry House, 1991.

Rupp, Rebecca. *Home Learning Year by Year : How to Design a Homeschool Curriculum from Preschool through High School*. 1st ed. New York: Three Rivers Press, 2000.

————. *The Complete Home Learning Sourcebook : The Essential Resource Guide for Homeschoolers, Parents, and Educators Covering Every Subject from Arithmetic to Zoology*. 1st ed. New York: Three Rivers Press, 1998.

Self-Education

Albert, David. *And the Skylark Sings with Me: Adventures in*

Homeschooling and Community-Based Education. Gabriola Island, BC: New Society Publishers, 1999.

———. *Homeschooling and the Voyage of Self-discovery : A Journey of Original Seeking*. Monroe Me.: Common Courage Press, 2003.

Griffith, Mary. *The Unschooling Handbook : How to Use the Whole World as your Child's Classroom*. Rocklin CA: Prima Pub., 1998.

Holt, John. *Instead of Education : Ways to Help People do Things Better*. 1st ed. Boulder CO: Sentient Publications, 2004.

———. *Learning All the Time*. Reading Mass.: Addison-Wesley, 1989.

Llewellyn, Grace. *The Teenage Liberation Handbook : How to Quit School and Get a Real Life and Education*. Eugene Or.: Lowry House, 1991.

Weldon, Laura Grace. *Free Range Learning: How Homeschooling Changes Everything*. Prescott, AZ: Hohm Press, 2010.

Charlotte Mason

Mason's own works are a bit difficult to read at first, so you may want to begin with one of these other authors. Also check out www.amblesideonline.org

Andreola, Karen. *A Charlotte Mason Companion : Personal Reflections on the Gentle Art of Learning*. Elkton Md.: Charlotte Mason Research & Supply, 1998.

Cooper, Elaine. *When Children Love to Learn : A Practical Application of Charlotte Mason's Philosophy for Today*. Wheaton Ill.: Crossway Books, 2004.

Levison, Catherine. *More Charlotte Mason Education : A Home Schooling How-To Manual*. New ed. Beverly Hills:

Champion Press, 2000.

Reading/Living Books

When my kids were little, I loved reading aloud to them from library picture books. But our reading aloud took on a whole new dimension when I discovered the *Five in a Row* series by Jane Claire Lambert and Becky Jane Lambert. Wonderful! You can find their books on their website: http://fiarhq.com/fiveinarow. info/index.html

Adler, Mortimer. *How to Read a Book*. Rev. and updated ed. New York: Simon and Schuster, 1972. — This book is not for teaching children how to read (decoding). It's more for teens and adults learning to get the most out of their reading.

Engelmann, Siegfried, Phyllis Haddox, and Elaine Bruner. *Teach Your Child to Read in 100 Easy Lessons*. 1st ed. New York: Simon & Schuster, 1986.

Fenner, Pamela. *Waldorf Student Reading List*. 3rd ed. Amesbury MA: Michaelmas Press, 1998.

Hunt, Gladys. *Honey for a Teen's Heart : Using Books to Communicate with Teens*. Grand Rapids Mich.: Zondervan, 2002.

Maslen, Bobby. *BOB Books: Beginning Readers*. Box Sets. New York: Scholastic, 2006.

Wilson, Elizabeth. *Books Children Love : A Guide to the Best Children's Literature*. Rev. ed. Wheaton Ill.: Crossway Books, 2002.

Learning Styles/Problems

Hannaford, Carla. *Smart Moves : Why Learning is Not All in Your Head*. Arlington Va.: Great Ocean Publishers,

1995.

Levine, Mel. *Mind at a Time (A)*. New York: Simon & ?Schuster, 2002.

Wahl, Mark. *Math for Humans : Teaching Math through 8 Intelligences*. Rev. ed. Langley Wash.: LivnLern Press, 1999.

Creativity

Gelb, Michael. *How to think like Leonardo Da Vinci : Seven Steps to Genius Every Day*. New York N.Y.: Dell Pub., 2000.

Michalko, Michael. *Cracking Creativity : The Secrets of Creative Genius*. Berkeley Calif.: Ten Speed Press, 2001.

Ruef, Kerry. *The Private Eye : Looking and Thinking by Analogy*. Seattle Wash.: Private Eye Project, 1992.

Writing

Bogart, Julie. *The Writer's Jungle*. West Chester, Ohio: Brave Writer, 2001.

Frank, Marjorie. *If You're Trying to Teach Kids How to Write, You've Gotta Have this Book!* Rev. ed. Nashville: Incentive Publications, 1995.

Kemper, Dave, and Write Source.; Great Source Education Group. *Writers INC : A Student Handbook for Writing and Learning*. Wilmington MA: Great Source Great Source Education Group, 2001.

White, Michael. *Fix-It! Grammar and Editing Made Easy with Classics*. Pleasantville N.Y.: Reader's Digest Association, 1995. — I also used other materials from the Institute for Excellence in Writing.

Wolf, Allan. *Immersed in Verse : An Informative, Slightly Irreverent & Totally Tremendous Guide to Living the Poet's Life*.

223

1st ed. New York: Lark Books, 2006.

Young, Sue, and Scholastic Inc. *The Scholastic Rhyming Dictionary*. New York: Scholastic Reference, 1997.

Zike, Dinah. *Dinah Zike's Big Book of Books and Activities : An Illustrated Guide for Teachers, Parents, and Anyone who Works with Kids!* San Antonio Tex.: Dinah-Might Activities, 2001.

Math

The Scholastic Professional Books Company is a really wonderful resource for hands-on games and activities. I used a lot of their math materials when my son rebelled against textbooks. He loved this stuff.

As my kids got older, we used the *Math-U-See* textbooks by Steve Demme and then *Teaching Textbooks* by Greg and Shawn Sabouri. Both have unique advantages. Check out their websites. I've also tried the acclaimed *Singapore Math* textbooks. I thought they were great but my kids didn't like the aesthetics. Again, there is so much more available now than what I have listed here. This is just to get you started.

Charlesworth, Eric. *225 Fantastic Facts Math Word Problems*. New York: Scholastic Professional Books, 2001.

Greenberg, Dan. *Funny & Fabulous Fraction Stories : 30 Reproducible Math Tales and Problems to Reinforce Important Fraction Skills*. New York: Scholastic Professional Books, 1996.

King, Julie, and Key Curriculum Press. *Key to Algebra*. Berkeley Calif.: Key Curriculum, 1990.

Lee, Martin. *Mega-Fun Fractions*. New York: Scholastic Professional Books, 2002.

Lotta, Chuck. *Fast & Fun Mental Math : 250 Quick Quizzes to*

Sharpen Math Skills Every Day of the School Year. New York: Scholastic Professional Books, 2000.

Rasmussen, Steven. *Key to Decimals*. Berkeley CA: Key Curriculum Project, 1985.

———. *Key to Percents*. Berkeley Calif.: Key Curriculum Press, 1988.

Schneider, Michael. *A Beginner's Guide to Constructing the Universe : The Mathematical Archetypes of Nature, Art, and Science*. 1st ed. New York NY: HarperPerennial, 1995.

Stenmark, Jean. *Family Math*. Berkeley CA: Lawrence Hall of Science University of California, 1986.

Thompson, Virginia. *Family Math, the Middle School Years : Algebraic Reasoning and Number Sense*. Berkeley CA: Lawrence Hall of Science University of California, 1998.

Vorderman, Carol. *How Math Works*. Pleasantville N.Y.: Reader's Digest Association, 1996.

Wahl, Mark. *A Mathematical Mystery Tour: Higher-Thinking Math Tasks*. Tucson Ariz.: Zephyr Press, 1988.

———. *Math for Humans : Teaching Math through 8 Intelligences*. Rev. ed. Langley Wash.: LivnLern Press, 1999.

Logic

Adler, Mortimer. *How to Read a Book*. Rev. and updated ed. New York: Simon and Schuster, 1972.

Bluedorn, Nathaniel. *The Fallacy Detective : Thirty-eight Lessons on How to Recognize Bad Reasoning*. 3rd ed. Muscatine Ia.: Christian Logic, 2009.

———. *The Thinking Toolbox : Thirty-five Lessons that will Build your Reasoning Skills*. Muscatine Iowa: Christian Logic, 2005.

Science

Ardley, Neil. *How Things Work*. Pleasantville N.Y.: Reader's Digest Association, 1995.

Burnie, David, and Reader's Digest Association. *How Nature Works*. Pleasantville N.Y.: Reader's Digest Association, 1991.

Caduto, Michael. *Keepers of Life : Discovering Plants through Native American stories and Earth Activities for Children*. 1st ed. Golden Colo.: Fulcrum Pub., 1998.

————. *Keepers of the Animals : Native American Stories and Wildlife Activities for Children*. Golden Colo.: Fulcrum Pub., 1991.

————. *Keepers of the Earth : Native American Stories and Environmental Activities for Children*. 1st ed. Golden Colo: Fulcrum Publ., 1997.

————. *Keepers of the Night : Native American Stories and Nocturnal Activities for Children*. Golden Colo.: Fulcrum Pub., 1994.

Couper, Heather. *How the Universe Works*. Pleasantville N.Y.: Reader's Digest Association, 1994.

Diehn, Gwen. *Science Crafts for Kids : 50 Fantastic Things to Invent & Create*. New York: Sterling, 1994.

Parker, Steve, and Reader's Digest Association. *How the Body Works*. Pleasantville N.Y.: Reader's Digest Association, 1994.

Ruef, Kerry. *The Private Eye : Looking and Thinking by Analogy*. Seattle Wash.: Private Eye Project, 1992.

Outdoor Activities

Beard, Daniel. *The American Boys Handy Book : What to Do and*

How to Do It. Centennial ed. Boston: D.R. Godine, 1983.

Brown, Tom. *Tom Brown's Field Guide to Nature and Survival for Children*. Berkley trade pbk. ed. New York: Berkley Books, 1989.

Caduto, Michael. *Keepers of Life : Discovering Plants through Native American stories and Earth Activities for Children*. 1st ed. Golden Colo.: Fulcrum Pub., 1998.

————. *Keepers of the Animals : Native American Stories and Wildlife Activities for Children*. Golden Colo.: Fulcrum Pub., 1991.

————. *Keepers of the Earth : Native American Stories and Environmental Activities for Children*. 1st ed. Golden Colo: Fulcrum Publ., 1997.

————. *Keepers of the Night : Native American Stories and Nocturnal Activities for Children*. Golden Colo.: Fulcrum Pub., 1994.

Diehn, Gwen. *Nature Crafts for Kids*. New York: Sterling Pub., 1992.

Hopman, Ellen. *Walking the World in Wonder : A Children's Herbal*. Rochester Vt.: Healing Arts Press, 2000.

Lovejoy, Sharon. *Roots, Shoots, Buckets & Boots*. New York: Workman Publishing Group, 1999.

Tierra, Lesley. *A Kid's Herbal Book*. San Francisco CA: Robert D. Reed Publishers, 2000.

Whitefeather, Willy. *Willy Whitefeather's Outdoor Survival Handbook for Kids*. Tucson: Harbinger House, 1990.

Having Fun

Beard, Daniel. *The American Boys Handy Book : What to Do and*

How to Do It. Centennial ed. Boston: D.R. Godine, 1983.

Blood, Peter. *Rise Up Singing : The Group-Singing Song Book*. Bethlehem, Pa. :: Sing Out Corp.,,, 1992.

Carey, Diana. *Festivals, Family and Food*. Gloucestershire: Hawthorne Press, 1982.

Cooper, Stephanie. *The Children's Year : Crafts and Clothes for Children and Parents to Make*. Stroud: Hawthorn, 1986.

Couper, Heather. *How the Universe Works*. Pleasantville N.Y.: Reader's Digest Association, 1994.

Diehn, Gwen. *Nature Crafts for Kids*. New York: Sterling Pub., 1992.

————. *Science Crafts for Kids : 50 Fantastic Things to Invent & Create*. New York: Sterling, 1994.

Gould, Roberta. *Making Cool Crafts & Awesome Art : A Kids' Treasure Trove of Fabulous Fun*. Charlotte Vt.: Williamson Pub., 1998.

Kealoha, Anna. *Trust the Children : A Manual and Activity Guide for Homeschooling and Alternative Learning*. Berkeley Calif.: Celestial Arts, 1995.

Kohl, MaryAnn. *Discovering Great Artists : Hands-on Art for Children in the Styles of the Great Masters*. Bellingham WA: Bright Ring Pub. Inc., 1996.

Lithgow, John. *A Lithgow Palooza! : 101 Ways to Entertain and Inspire your Kids*. New York: Simon & Schuster, 2004.

Pinchuk, Amy. *Make Amazing Toy and Game Gadgets*. 1st ed. [New York N.Y.]: HarperCollinsPublishers, 2001.

————. *Make Cool Gadgets for your Room*. 1st ed. [New York NY]: HarperCollinsPublishers, 2001.

Ruef, Kerry. *The Private Eye : Looking and Thinking by Analogy*.

Seattle Wash.: Private Eye Project, 1992.

Zike, Dinah. *Dinah Zike's Big Book of Books and Activities : An Illustrated Guide for Teachers, Parents, and Anyone who Works with Kids!* San Antonio Tex.: Dinah-Might Activities, 2001.

Getting Ready for College

Berger, Larry. *Up Your Score : The Underground Guide to the SAT.* 2009th ed. New York: Workman Pub., 2008.

Dennis, Jeanne. *Homeschooling High School : Planning Ahead for College Admission.* 2nd ed. Lynwood WA: Emerald Books, 2004.

King, Elizabeth. *Outsmarting the SAT : An Expert Tutor Reveals her Proven Techniques, Strategies, and Confidence-Building Exercises that Will Maximize your Score.* Berkeley: Ten Speed Press, 2008.

Llewellyn, Grace. *The Teenage Liberation Handbook : How to Quit School and Get a Real Life and Education.* Eugene Or.: Lowry House, 1991.

Successful Habits / Setting Goals

Covey, Stephen. *The Seven Habits of Highly Effective Families : Building a Beautiful Family Culture in a Turbulent World.* New York: Golden Books, 1997.

———. *The Seven Habits of Highly Effective People : Restoring the Character Ethic.* 1st ed. New York: Fireside Book, 1990.

Hill, Napoleon, and Arthur R. Dr. Pell. *Think and Grow Rich.* New York NY: Penguin, 2005.

Marden, Orison Swett. *Making Life a Masterpiece.* Elibron Classics. Adamant Media Corporation, 2005.

Shimoff, Marci. *Happy for No Reason : 7 Steps to Being Happy from the Inside Out.* 1st ed. New York: Free Press, 2008.

Parenting/Discipline

Cline, Foster. *Parenting with Love and Logic : Teaching Children Responsibility.* Colorado Springs Colo.: Navpress, 1990.

Covey, Stephen. *The Seven Habits of Highly Effective Families : Building a Beautiful Family Culture in a Turbulent World.* New York: Golden Books, 1997.

Notes

Endnotes: Chapter One

1   Pearl Buck, *My Several Worlds: A Personal Record* (New York: The John Day Company, 1954), 61.
2   Laurence Bergreen, *Louis Armstrong: An Extravagant Life* (New York: Broadway Books), 103-104.
3   Gary Giddins, *Satchmo: The Genius of Louis Armstrong* (Da Capo Press, 1988), 32.

Endnotes: Chapter Two

1   Victor Goertzel, *Cradles of Eminence : Childhoods of More than Seven Hundred Famous Men and Women : The Complete Original Text* (Scottsdale AZ: Great Potential Press, 2004), 262.
2   Alfie Kohn, *What Does it Mean To Be Well Educated?* (Boston: Beacon Press, 2004), 6.
3   Napoleon Hill, *Think and Grow Rich : The Landmark Bestseller—Now revised and updated for the 21st century* (New York: Jeremy P. Tarcher/Penguin, 2005), 80.
4   Ibid., 86.
5   John Muir, *The Story of My Boyhood and Youth* (San Francisco CA: Sierra Club Books, 1988), 134.

6   Ansel Adams and Mary Street Alinder, *Ansel Adams: An Autobiography* (Boston: Little, Brown and Company, 1985), 17.

7   Mary Leakey, *Disclosing the Past: An Autobiography* (Garden City NY: Doubleday & Company, 1984), 32.

8   Ibid.

9   Neil Baldwin, *Edison: Inventing the Century* (New York: Hyperion, 1995), 25.

10   Ibid., 26.

11   Robyn Weaver, *Alexander Graham Bell* (San Diego: Lucent Books, 2000), 21.

12   Ibid., 22.

13   C.S. Lewis, *Surprised by Joy: The Shape of My Early Life* (New York: Harcourt, Brace & World, 1955), 144.

14   Ibid., 144-145.

Endnotes: Chapter Three

1   Norman R. Augustine, *Is America Falling Off the Flat Earth?* (Washington D.C.: The National Academies Press, 2007), 6.

2   Patrick Gonzales, "Highlights from TRIMMS 2007: Mathematics and Science Achievement of U.S. Fourth- and Eighth-Grade Students in an International Context" (National Center for Education Statistics, 2009); available from <http://nces.ed.gov/pubs97/timss/97198.asp>

3   R.D. Shelton and P. Foland, "The Race for World Leadership of Science and Technology: Status and Forecasts" (The Alliance For Science and Technology Research in America, 2009); available from <http://www.aboutastra.org/latest_news/10-27-2009_world-leadership-science.asp>

4   Central Intelligence Agency, "Country Comparison: Education Expenditures" (Central Intelligence Agency, 2010); available from <https://www.cia.gov/library/publications/the-world-factbook/rankorder/2206rank.html>

5   Orison Swett Marden, *How They Succeeded: Life Stories of Successful Men Told by Themselves* (Whitefish, Montana: Kessinger Publishing, 2003), 274-75.

6   Richard Meryman, *Andrew Wyeth: A Secret Life* (Harper Collins Publishers, 1996), 50.

Endnotes: Chapter Four

1   Janet Morgan, *Agatha Christie: A Biography* (New York: Alfred A. Knopf, 1984), 20.

2   Raymond and Dorothy Moore, *Better Late Than Early: A New Approach to Your Child's Education* (Camas, WA: Reader's Digest Press), 84.

3   Ibid., 78.

4   Lewis, 10.

5   Charlotte Mason, *School Education* (Wheaton, IL: Tyndale House, 1989), 228.

6   Ibid., 177.

7   Ibid.

8   Charlotte Mason, *A Philosophy of Education* (Wheaton, IL: Tyndale House, 1989), 105.

9   Orison Swett Marden, *Making Life a Masterpiece* (New York: Thomas Y. Crowell Company, 1916), 131.

Endnotes: Chapter Five

1   Richard Florida, *The Rise of the Creative Class: How it's Transforming Work, Leisure, Community and Everyday Life* (New York: Basic Books, 2004), 44.

2   Ibid., 5.

3   Ibid., 45-46.

4   Ibid., 47.

5   Margaret Lane, *The Tale of Beatrix Potter: A Biography* (London: Frederick Warne & Co., 1968), 52.

6   Denis Brian, *The Curies: A Biography of the Most Con-*

troversial Family in Science (Hoboken, NJ: John Wiley & Sons, Inc., 2005), 7-8.

7   Ibid., 4.

8   Ibid.

9   Angeline Stoll Lillard, *Montessori: The Science Behind the Genius* (New York: Oxford University Press), 172.

10   John Briggs, *Fire in the Crucible: Understanding the Process of Creative Genius* (Grand Rapids, MI: Phanes Press, 2000), 210.

11   Lillard, 172.

12   Ibid., 179.

13   Kohn, 111.

14   Daniel Goleman et al., *The Creative Spirit* (New York: A Dutton Book, Penguin Group, 1992), 66.

15   Lewis, 34.

16   Meryman, 44-45.

17   Ibid., 83.

18   Ibid., 44.

19   Howard Gardner, *Creating Minds: An Anatomy of Creativity Seen Through the Lives of Freud, Einstein, Picasso, Stravinsky, Eliot, Graham and Gandhi* (New York: Basic Books, 1993), 105.

20   Ibid., 145.

21   Goleman et al., 57.

22   Gardner, 31.

23   Ibid., 90-92.

Endnotes: Chapter Six

1   Malcolm X and Alex Haley, *The Autobiography of Malcolm X* (Pennsylvania: Chelsea House Publishers, 1996), 37.

2   Walter Dean Myers, *By Any Means Necessary: Malcolm X* (New York: Scholastic, 1993), 67-68.

3   Daniel Coyle, *The Talent Code : Greatness isn't Born: it's Grown, Here's How* (New York: Bantam Books, 2009), 124.

4   Ibid., 105.

5   Ibid.

6   John Brockman, ed., *Curious Minds: How a Child Becomes a Scientist* (New York: Pantheon Books, 2004), 184.

Endnotes: Chapter Seven

1   Marden, *Making Life a Masterpiece*, 298.

2   Baldwin, 20.

3   Hill, 56.

4   Marden, *How They Succeeded*, 280.

5   Ibid.

6   William Manchester, *American Caesar: Douglas MacArthur 1880 - 1964* (Boston: Little, Brown and Company, 1978), 41.

7   Adams and Alinder, 21.

8   Theodore Roosevelt, *Theodore Roosevelt: an Autobiography* (Macmillan, 1913), 8.

9   Goertzel, 205.

10   Dave Thomas, "Humble Beginnings" (2003); available from <http://www.wendys.com/dave/>

11   Margaret Mead, *Blackberry Winter: My Earlier Years* (New York: William Morrow and Company, 1972), 46-47.

12   Baldwin, 222.

13   Ibid., 222-223.

14   Ibid., 247.

15   Ibid., 287-288.

16   Ibid., 259.

17   Ibid., 379.

18   Marden, *Making Life a Masterpiece*, 225-226.

Endnotes: Chapter Eight

1   Marden, *Making Life a Masterpiece*, 89.

2   Marden, *How they Succeeded*, 237-238.

3   David Nasaw, *Andrew Carnegie* (New York: The Penguin Press, 2006), 38.

4   Ibid., 22.

5   Jeanette Mirsky and Allan Nevins, *The World of Eli Whitney* (New York: The MacMillan Company, 1952), 9.

6   Charlotte Mason, *Home Education* (Wheaton, IL: Tyndale House, 1989), 324.

7   Ibid., 328-329.

8   Maria Montessori, *Spontaneous Activity in Education* (Schocken Books, 1965), 189.

Endnotes: Chapter Nine

1   Steve Jobs Stanford Commencement Speech 2005; available from <http://www.youtube.com/watch#!v=UF8uR6Z6KLc&feature=related>.

2   Carolyn G. Heilbrun, *The Education of a Woman: The Life of Gloria Steinem* (New York: The Dial Press, 1995), 21.

Endnotes: Chapter Ten

1   Bernard B. Kerik, *The Lost Son: A Life in Pursuit of Justice* (New York: Regan Books, 2001), 42.

2   Ibid., 52-53.

3   Muir, 19.

4   Marden, *How they Succeeded*, 187.

Endnotes: Chapter Eleven

1   David McCullough, *Mornings on Horseback: The Story of an Extraordinary Family, A Vanished Way of Life, and the Unique Child Who Became Theodore Roosevelt* (New York: Simon & Shuster, 2003), 37.

2   Ibid., 165.

3   Mason, *A Philosophy of Education*, 109.

4   Mead, 90.

5   Brockman, 10.
6   Ibid., 11.
7   Ibid., 46.
8   Goertzel, 45.

Endnotes: Chapter Twelve

1   H.W. Brands, *The First American: The Life and Times of Benjamin Franklin* (New York: Anchor Books, 2000), 97-98.
2   Mason, *Home Education*, 136.
3   Charlotte Mason, *Formation of Character* (Wheaton, IL: Tyndale House, 1989), 60-61.
4   Ibid., 66.
5   Ibid., 28.
6   Ibid., 29.
7   Ibid., 30.
8   Coyle, 40-41.
9   Ibid., 168-169.
10   Ibid., 170.
11   Lewis, 112.

Endnotes: Chapter Thirteen

1   William Roscoe Thayer, *Theodore Roosevelt: An Intimate Biography* (New York: Houghton Mifflin Company 1919), 262-263.
2   Center for Science, Mathematics, and Engineering Education, "Inquiry and the National Scence Education Standards: A Guide for Teaching and Learning" (The National Academies Press, 2000), available from <http://www.nap.edu/openbook.php?record_id=9596&page=115>, 115.
3   Baldwin, 19.
4   Mason, *Home Education*, 43-44.
5   Ibid., 45.
6   Marden, *Making Life a Masterpiece*, 104-105.

Endnotes: Chapter Fourteen

1   Thomas G. West, *Thinking Like Einstein: Returning to Our Visual Roots With the Emerging Revolution in Computer Information Visualization* (New York: Prometheus Books, 2004), 84.

2   Ibid., 156.

3   Ibid., 173.

4   Ibid., 172.

5   Jon Katz, *Geeks: How Two Lost Boys Rode the Internet out of Idaho* (New York: Villard, 2000), xxxviii - xl.

6   Brockman, 178.

7   Ursula K. LeGuin, "Biography - Frequently Asked Questions," available from <http://www.ursulakleguin.com/FAQ.html#Childhood>

8   Goleman et al., 92.

Endnotes: Chapter Fifteen

1   Brockman, 209.

2   Ibid., 225.

Bibliography

Adams, Ansel, and Mary Street Alinder. *Ansel Adams: An Autobiography*. Boston: Little, Brown and Company, 1985.

Augustine, Norman R. *Is America Falling Off the Flat Earth?* Washington DC: The National Academies Press, 2007.

Axelrod, Alan. *Patton: A Biography*. New York: Palgrave MacMillan, 2006.

Baldwin, Neil. *Edison: Inventing the Century*. New York: Hyperion, 1995.

Bateson, Mary Catherine. *With a Daughter's Eye: A Memoir of Margaret Mead and Gregory Bateson*. New York: William Morrow and Company, 1984.

Bergreen, Laurence. *As Thousands Cheer: The Life of Irving Berlin*. New York: Viking, 1990.

Bergreen, Laurence. *Louis Armstrong: An Extravagant Life*. New York: Broadway Books, 1997.

Birch, Beverley. *Guglielmo Marconi: Radio Pioneer*. Woodbridge, CT: Blackbirch Press, Inc., 2001.

Brands, H.W. *The First American: The Life and Times of Benjamin Franklin*. New York: Anchor Books, 2000.

Brian, Denis. *The Curies: A Biography of the Most Controversial Family in Science*. Hoboken, New Jersey: John Wiley & Sons, Inc., 2005.

Briggs, John. *Fire in the Crucible: Understanding the Process of Creative Genius*. Grand Rapids, MI: Phanes Press, 2000.

Brockman, John, edited by. *Curious Minds: How a Child Becomes a Scientist*. New York: Pantheon Books, 2004.

Buck, Pearl S. *My Several Worlds: A Personal Record*. New York: The John Day Company, 1954.

Center for Science, Mathematics, and Engineering Education. "Inquiry and the National Scence Education Standards: A Guide for Teaching and Learning (2000)." The National Academies Press, 2000. <http://www.nap.edu/openbook.php?record_id=9596&page=115>.

Central Intelligence Agency. "Country Comparison: Education Expenditures." Central Intelligence Agency, August 2010. <https://www.cia.gov/library/publications/the-world-factbook/rankorder/2206rank.html>.

Cooke, Nathalie. *Margaret Atwood: A Biography*. Toronto, Ontario: ECW Press, 1998.

Coyle, Daniel. *The Talent Code : Greatness Isn't Born : It's Grown, Here's How*. New York: Bantam Books, 2009.

Cremin, Lawrence A. *American Education: The Colonial Experience 1607-1783*. New York: Harper & Row, Publishers, 1970.

Florida, Richard. *The Rise of the Creative class : and How it's Transforming Work, Leisure, Community and Everyday Life*. New York NY: Basic Books, 2004.

Gardner, Howard. *Creating Minds: An Anatomy of Creativity Seen Through the Lives of Freud, Einstein, Picasso, Stravinsky, Eliot, Graham and Gandhi*. New York: Basic

Books, a Division of Harper Collins Publishers, Inc., 1993.

Gelb, Michael. *How to Think Like Leonardo Da Vinci : Seven Steps to Genius Every Day.* New York N.Y.: Dell Pub., 2000.

Gelb, Michael. *Discover your Genius : How to Think Like History's Ten Most Revolutionary Minds.* 1st ed. New York: Quill, 2003.

Giddins, Gary. Satchmo: *The Genius of Louis Armstrong.* Da Capo Press, 1988.

Goertzel, Victor and Mildred George, updated by Ted George Goertzel and Ariel M. W. Hansen. *Cradles of Eminence: Childhoods of More Than Seven Hundred Famous Men and Women : the complete original text.* 2nd ed. Scottsdale Ariz.: Great Potential Press, 2004.

Goleman, Daniel, Paul Kaufman, and Michael Ray. *The Creative Spirit.* New York NY: A Dutton Book, Penguin Group, 1992.

Golley, John. *Genesis of the Jet: Frank Whittle and the Invention of the Jet Engine.* UK: Airlife Publishing, 1996.

Gonzalez, Patrick. "Highlights from TRIMSS 2007: Mathematics and Science Achievement of U.S. Fourth- and Eighth-Grade Students in an International Context." National Center for Education Statistics, September 2009. <http://nces.ed.gov/pubs97/timss/97198.asp>.

Gould, Jean. *Robert Frost: The Aim Was Song.* New York: Dodd, Mead & Company, 1964.

Harris, Theodore F. *Pearl S. Buck: A Biography.* New York: The John Day Company, 1969.

Heckscher, August. *Woodrow Wilson: A Biography.* New York: Charles Scribner's Sons, 1991.

Heilbrun, Carolyn G. *The Education of a Woman: The Life of Gloria Steinem*. New York: The Dial Press, 1995.

Hill, Napoleon. *Think and Grow Rich : the Landmark Bestseller--now revised and updated for the 21st century*. 1st ed. New York: Jeremy P. Tarcher/Penguin, 2005.

Howard, Fred. *Wilbur and Orville: A Biography of the Wright Brothers*. New York: Alfred A. Knopf, 1987.

Huxtable, Ada Louise. *Frank Lloyd Wright*. New York: Viking Penguin Group, 2004.

Johnson, Edgar. *Charles Dickens: His Tragedy and Triumph. Vol. 1*. New York NY: Simon and Schuster, 1952.

Katz, Jon. *Geeks: How Two Lost Boys Rode the Internet out of Idaho*. New York: Villard, 2000.

Kerik, Bernard B. *The Lost Son: A Life in Pursuit of Justice*. New York: Regan Books, 2001.

Kohn, Alfie. *Punished by Rewards: The Trouble With Gold Stars, Incentive Plans, A's, Praise and Other Bribes*. New York: Houghton Mifflin, 1993.

Kohn, Alfie. *What Does it Mean To Be Well Educated?* Boston: Beacon Press, 2004.

Kramer, Barbara. *Dave Thomas: Honesty Pays. Awesome Values in Famous Lives*. Berkeley Heights, NJ: Enslow Publishers, Inc., 2005.

Lane, Margaret. *The Tale of Beatrix Potter: A Biography*. London: Frederick Warne & Co. LTD, 1968.

Leakey, Mary. *Disclosing the Past: An Autobiography*. Garden City, New York: Doubleday & Company, 1984.

LeGuin, Ursula K. "Biography - Frequently Asked Questions." Ursula K. LeGuin, n.d. <http://www.ursulakleguin.com/FAQ.html#Childhood>.

Lewis, C.S. *Surprised by Joy: The Shape of My Early Life*. New York: Harcourt, Brace & World, Inc., 1955.

Lillard, Angeline Stoll. *Montessori: the Science behind the Genius*. New York: Oxford University Press, 2005.

Loving, Jerome. *Walt Whitman: The Song of Himself*. Berkeley and Los Angeles, CA: University of California Press, 1999.

Manchester, William. *American Caesar: Douglas MacArthur 1880 - 1964*. Boston: Little, Brown and Company, 1978.

Marden, Orison Swett. *How they Succeeded: Life Stories of Successful Men Told by Themselves*, Whitefish Mont.: Kessinger Publishing, 2003.

———. *Making Life a Masterpiece*. Elibron Classics. New York NY: Thomas Y. Crowell Company, 1916.

Mason, Charlotte. *A Philosophy of Education*. Wheaton Ill.: Tyndale House, 1989.

———. *Formation of Character*. Wheaton Ill.: Tyndale House, 1989.

———. *Home Education*. Wheaton Ill.: Tyndale House, 1989.

———. *School Education*. Wheaton Ill.: Tyndale House, 1989.

———. *Parents and Children*. Wheaton Ill.: Tyndale House, 1989.

———. *Ourselves*. Wheaton Ill.: Tyndale House, 1989.

McCullough, David. *Mornings on Horseback: The Story of an Extraordinary Family, A Vanished Way of Life, and the Unique Child Who Became Theodore Roosevelt*. New York: Simon & Schuster, 2003.

Mead, Margaret. *Blackberry Winter: My Earlier Years*. New York: William Morrow and Company, 1972.

Meryman, Richard. *Andrew Wyeth: A Secret Life*. Harper Collins Publishers, 1996.

Mirsky, Jeanette, and Allan Nevins. *The World of Eli Whitney*. New York: The MacMillan Company, 1952.

Montessori, Maria. *Spontaneous Activity in Education*. Edited by John McDermott. Translated by Florence Simm Onds. Schocken Books, 1965.

Moore, Raymond S., and Dorothy N. Moore. *Better Late Than Early: A New Approach to Your Child's Education*. Camas, WA: Reader's Digest Press, 1975.

Morgan, Janet. *Agatha Christie: A Biography*. New York: Alfred A. Knopf, 1984.

Muir, John. *The Story of My Boyhood and Youth*. San Francisco CA: Sierra Club Books, 1988.

Myers, Walter Dean. *By Any Means Necessary: Malcolm X*. New York: Scholastic, 1993.

Nasaw, David. *Andrew Carnegie*. New York: The Penguin Press, 2006.

Roosevelt, Theodore. *Theodore Roosevelt: an Autobiography*. Macmillan, 1913.

Spring, Joel. *The American School: 1642-1985*. New York: Longman, Inc., 1986.

Shelton, R.D., and P. Foland. "The Race for World Leadership of Science and Technology: Status and Forecasts." The Alliance For Science and Technology Research in America, October 27, 2009. <http://www.aboutastra. org/latest_news/10-27-2009_world-leadership-science. asp>.

Steve Jobs Stanford Commencement Speech 2005, 2005. <http://www.youtube.com/watch#!v=UF8uR6Z6KLc&

feature=related>.

Thayer, William Roscoe. *Theodore Roosevelt: an Intimate Biography*. New York: Houghton Mifflin Company, 1919.

Thomas, Dave. "Humble Beginnings." Dave Thomas, 2003. <http://www.wendys.com/dave/>.

Wadsworth, Ginger. *John Muir: Wilderness Protector*. Minneapolis: Lerner Publications Company, 1992.

Wead, Doug. *The Raising of a President: The Mothers and Fathers of Our Nation's Leaders*. New York: Atria Books, 2005.

Weaver, Robyn. *Alexander Graham Bell*. San Diego: Lucent Books, 2000.

West, Thomas G. *Thinking Like Einstein: Returning to Our Visual Roots With the Emerging Revolution in Computer Information Visualization*. New York: Prometheus Books, 2004.

Williams, Robert C. *Horace Greeley: Champion of American Freedom*. New York: New York University Press, 2006.

Wilson, A.N. *C.S. Lewis: A Biography*. New York: W.W. Norton & Company, 1990.

Woods, Paul A. *Quentin Tarantino: The Film Geek Files*. London: Plexus, 2005.

X, Malcolm, and Alex Haley. *The Autobiography of Malcolm X*. Pennsylvania: Chelsea House Publishers, 1996.

Index

A

B

C

S

T

U

V

W

X

CPSIA information can be obtained at www.ICGtesting.com
Printed in the USA
LVOW091527260112

265717LV00002B/84/P